Richard Harries, who is Dean of King's College, London, was born in 1936 and educated at Selwyn College, Cambridge, and Cuddesdon Theological College. A priest of the Church of England, he has spent much of his ministry in parish life including six years in Hampstead and nine years as Vicar of Fulham (All Saints). He was on the staff of Wells Theological College and retains an interest in ordination training as Chairman of the Southwark Ordination Course. His main academic interests are the relationship between religion and literature and Christian Ethics. He has written widely on the ethics of war, revolution and the nuclear issue.

Mr Harries is the author of ten books, including *Turning to Prayer* and *Being a Christian*. He recently combined with Kallistos Ware and George Every to produce *Seasons of the Spirit*, a unique Anglican, Roman Catholic, Orthodox collection of readings relating to the Church's year, East and West. He writes for a number of papers and journals including a weekly column for "The Church Times". He is also a regular contributor to Television and Radio, being best known for his BBC Radio 4 "Prayer for the Day", which he has broadcast on Friday mornings since 1973. In 1984 he was voted tenth in the BBC's "Man of the Year" competition.

Mr Harries is married to a doctor. They have two children, a son studying medicine at Cambridge and a daughter still at school.

Richard Harries

PRAYER AND THE PURSUIT OF HAPPINESS

Foreword by the Archbishop of Canterbury

Collins
FOUNT PAPERBACKS
in association with
Faith Press

First published by Fount Paperbacks, London
in association with Faith Press, in 1985

Copyright © Richard Harries 1985

Made and printed in Great Britain by
William Collins Sons & Co. Ltd, Glasgow

For Bishop Simeon CR, Pamela Warnes,
the staff of St Mary's Cathedral, Johannesburg,
and all those struggling for human fulfilment
in South Africa

Contents

Foreword

by the Archbishop of Canterbury

In *Prayer and the Pursuit of Happiness* Richard Harries displays his rare and admirable gifts as a Christian teacher and communicator. He has the facility to render the profoundest truths intelligible and to invest the stale and familiar with fresh meaning and relevance. Beneath the surface lies a wealth of theological understanding which, enlivened by the insights of literature, never fails to speak to the anxieties and aspirations of the human heart.

The pursuit of happiness dominates our lives and its promise comes in many forms. In the face of today's vain and elusive offers of happiness through self-indulgent hedonism, sentimentality or material affluence the Christian can be tempted to turn his back on the world and adopt instead a more austere and ascetic way of life.

This book makes it clear that such a short-cut is just as illusory. Our longing for happiness and fulfilment, success and security, are God-given, and not to be despised. "God wants us to want." The Christian calling is not to deprive ourselves but rather to direct our desires towards God in a life which has devotion, love and prayer at its heart. This is the way to the deepest, most satisfying peace and happiness of all – the happiness of God, the peace which the world alone cannot give.

Lambeth Palace   Robert Cantuar:
June 1984

Introduction

In the summer of 1982 I was invited to give some talks at St Mary's Cathedral, Johannesburg. It was in those talks that I first began to explore the themes developed in this book. Since then they have been shaped up through contact with various parish groups.

I am very grateful to Mrs Gillian Ryeland for typing the script with her usual good will and efficiency.

Richard Harries
May 1984

1.

Starting Where You Want

In Barbara Pym's novel *Quartet in Autumn* a character called Norman goes to visit his brother-in-law, Ken, in hospital:

> Now that his sister was dead there was no direct link between him and Ken, and Norman felt pleasantly virtuous at going to see him. He has no one, he thought, for the only child of the marriage had emigrated to New Zealand. In fact Ken did have somebody, a woman friend whom he expected to marry, but she did not visit on the same day as Norman. "Let him come on his own," they had said to each other, "for after all he has no one and the visit will be a bit of company for him."[1]

In this hospital visit both Norman and Ken think that they are doing some good to the other. This is encouraging. It is a ground of hope that there are millions of people like Norman and Ken who want to be of use to others. Yet, as Barbara Pym makes clear, in a way which is perceptive without being cynical, there is a great deal more going on in that hospital visit than the two men are aware of.

Most obviously there is the "pleasantly virtuous" feeling that Norman gets out of visiting someone to whom he has no direct responsibility. Then there is the reluctance of Ken to have good done to him. He and his friend think of Norman as the one in real need, the lonely one, whom they must try to help. Norman is not aware of this, nor is it a thought he would have found appealing. When we are doing good to others, particularly when it is of an obvious kind like visiting

13

a helpless person in hospital, there is a sense in which we are in a position of power over them. Conversely, when we are receiving the ministrations of someone else, we are vulnerable. This is one of the reasons why sometimes we would rather help than be helped.

Norman and Ken and the rest of us have many wants and needs we do not fully admit to ourselves, let alone to anyone else. There is self-deception and collusion in mutual deception. Like all deception this is both unsatisfactory and dangerous. Even the hospital visit did not go very well for Norman: "The evening had exhausted him and he did not even feel that he had done Ken much good." One of the reasons it did not go well was that Norman was fleeing his own inner discontent (of which irritability was the outer sign) by doing good. I remember as a curate setting out one afternoon to do some visits and suddenly being aware that I was in fact going out to look for someone more miserable than myself to comfort. I continued on my way but the awareness that in visiting I was meeting my own needs as well as those of others did, I think, make the eventual encounters more satisfactory.

Self-deception not only brings edginess and a jarring note into our relationships; it can bring disaster. A public figure was once up in court for an act of indecency that was humiliating and totally out of character. This person was a highly intellectual, principled and disciplined person. After the incident he wrote: "I have been deeply pained for about four years and probably trying to transmute my discontents too directly to spiritual ends." That is just what he was doing. But our needs cannot be ground down in that manner, and if we make the attempt they make themselves known and often trip us up in so doing.

If asked, no doubt both Norman and Ken would have said that Christianity was about being "unselfish". The starting point and assumption of this book is rather different. We are a bundle of wants and this is how God has made us. So God wants us to want. He wants us to want things not only for other people but for ourselves as well.

The Christian who takes our wanting more seriously than almost anything else is the seventeenth century poet and spiritual writer, Thomas Traherne. According to him there is want within God himself:

> Infinite want is the very ground and cause of infinite treasure. It is incredible, yet very plain: want is the fountain of all his fullness. Want in God is a treasure to us. For had there been no need he would not have created the world, nor made us. But he wanted Angels and men, images, companions.[2]

Furthermore, God has created us not only with the capacity to want but with the capacity to want more and more; with an insatiable desire.

> It is of the nobility of man's soul that he is insatiable, for he hath a benefactor so prone to give, that he delighteth in us for asking. Do not your inclinations tell you that the world is yours? Do you not covet all? Do you not long to have it; to enjoy it; to overcome it? To what end do men gather riches, but to multiply more and more?[3]

Our problem is not that we want but that we don't want enough. We are satisfied with hoarding a few treasures when the whole universe is ours. "You must want like a God, that you may be satisfied like God."[4] So our wants are not to be ignored or trodden down or rejected as "selfish". They are vital.

> Wants are the bands and cements between God and us . . . From eternity it was requisite that we should want.

We could never else have enjoyed anything: Our own wants are treasures.[5]

Although Traherne strikes many modern Christians as idiosyncratic (though beautiful), his starting point is similar to that of most Christians in the Catholic and Pre-Reformation tradition. For Thomas Aquinas, as for Aristotle, it was basic that we are all seeking happiness. For various reasons, mainly a mixture of Protestant moralism and Kantian philosophy, we shy away from the idea that we are all seeking happiness and that this is both natural and good. Our search for happiness needs once more to be affirmed as the proper place to begin.

During this century the most forceful attack on the notion that our search for happiness is the proper place to begin has come from the Swedish theologian Anders Nygren. He argued that there is a total opposition between *agape*, self-forgetful love, which seeks only the good of the other, and *eros*, which is the self seeking the highest form of goodness, truth and beauty. He believed that eros came from Platonism and is essentially alien to Christianity. His argument is considered in more detail in the last chapter on love.[6]

Children who are always saying "I want" – I want this or I want that – are usually discouraged. Perhaps that is the reason we are suspicious of any theology that begins with, and affirms, the fact that we are a bundle of wants. Yet, whatever we feel about children who are always saying "I want", our attitude to others who state their wants is sometimes more positive. We admire a person who is quite clear what he or she wants to do with their life. "I want to be a musician" or "I want to marry and have children." We admire and envy people who are as clear and single-minded as that. It seems better to be like them than our usual undecided, half-hearted muddle. Charles Darwin had an interest in natural history from childhood. It was an interest he pursued for its own sake with delight, passion and assiduity. He performed in a mediocre manner at school. He dropped out of medical studies. He gave up the idea of being a clergyman. Eventually, as a result of his voyage on *The Beagle*, he found himself fully employed doing what he had always been groping his way towards. Darwin was lucky. Few then and few now are in a position to put their life at the disposal of their major interest. More important, few of us have the capacity to be that single-minded. For there was something admirable about Darwin's life, not simply its achievement, but in the way he was able to do what he most deeply wanted to do.

Children who are always saying "I want" are tedious. Another reason why we are suspicious of the whole idea of "wanting" is that our adult wants are often rather crude: "I want to be a millionaire" or "I want sex." Yet a person who is serious about what he wants, who is determined to be a millionaire, for example, and who sets about it in an intelligent and whole-hearted way has a stature which those of us who stand on the touch-lines of life can recognize and envy. A person who is seriously dedicated to becoming a millionaire is a tragic figure, and in all tragic figures there is an element of distorted greatness.

God has made us as creatures able to want; able to want like gods. Indeed part of what it means to be made in the image of God is that we are able to want. Animals have needs. We have not only needs but wants. Needs and wants are related but different. Sometimes they coincide and at other times they do not. We all have needs such as the need for food, for sleep and for attention. These needs become transmuted into wants when they become conscious. "I need some food" becomes "I want food." The mind and will become united in concerted action. It is true that not all wants reflect real needs. Yet they are often related in some

way even though in a distorted form. "I need six months off
on a tropical island" may not reflect an actual need but it is
clearly related to a need of some kind which may come to be
expressed in a different want. On reflection it may turn into
"I want to work less hard" or "I want to re-order the
priorities in my life" or even "I want to find some peace of
mind".

We begin life as a bundle of needs. As we become
conscious these become converted into a series of consciously
experienced and stated wants. Growing up is a process in
which our wanting becomes matured and refined. It has been
said that when we die all that will happen to us is that we will
hear the words, "You can have what you want". The
question is, what, by then, will we have come to want?

Edward Thomas wrote a poem in which he considered all
the gifts he might bestow on his daughter Helen:

> I would give you youth,
> All kinds of loveliness and truth,
> A clear eye as good as mine,
> Lands, waters, flowers, wine.[7]

The poet comes in the end to what he considers the best gift
of all:

> If I could choose
> Freely in that great treasure-house
> Anything from any shelf,
> I would give you back yourself,
> And power to discriminate
> What you want and want it not too late.

The poem suggests that the greatest gift we can receive is our
very self, the person we are, with the power to discriminate,
to know what we want and want it not too late.

There are certain goals or values or states of mind that we all seek. Happiness, peace, fulfilment, security, success and love are the most obvious ones. As stated in a list like that, these are only words. The question is, what is meant by those words, and how do we reach that which the words indicate? Nevertheless, that we are all seeking happiness, or some meaning of that word, is obvious; similarly with the other values on the list.

Writers and guides on prayer are fond of saying "Begin where you are". In other words, they say, do not try to pretend you are someone else or that you are at a different stage of prayer. Begin with yourself, as you are. This means, beginning with the wants we actually have; starting where we want.

There is an intimate connection between wanting and prayer. For prayer is a kind of wanting before God. Furthermore, it is above all in and through prayer that our wants become deepened and refined. T. S. Eliot wrote about "The purification of the motive in the ground of our beseeching".[8] Our beseeching is prayer and the ground of our beseeching is God himself. It is in prayer, in God, that we come to want differently.

✠

Grant us, O God,
the power to discriminate,
to know what we want and want it not too late.

NOTES

1. Barbara Pym, *Quartet in Autumn*, Granada 1980, p. 12.
2. *Centuries, Poems and Thanksgivings*, ed. H.M. Margoliouth, Vol. I, Century 42, spelling modernized.
3. ibid, Century 22.
4. ibid, Century 44.
5. ibid, Century 22.
6. Recently Helen Oppenheimer has published an excellent book, whose starting point is the same as this one, *The Hope of Happiness*. She deals with some of the more philosophical questions, which are not the concern of this book: but on the whole Nygren's view has prevailed and there has been very little Christian writing in recent years on the assumption that our desire for Happiness is good and God-given.
7. Edward Thomas "And You, Helen", in *Collected Poems*, Faber 1974 edition, p. 39.
8. *Little Gidding* III.

FOR DISCUSSION

1. Is it "selfish" to take our personal wants into account?

2. Is it possible to justify, from a Christian point of view, an approach to life that begins from the assumption that we are creatures who want?

3. What are the basic goods and values that human beings desire?

2.

Happiness

Happiness Matters and Can Be Found

As a curate I went once to visit an American lady. We were sitting talking on the sofa when she suddenly turned to me, looked me in the eyes and said, "Are you happy?" She did not mean, was I happy sitting with her at that moment. She meant, was I happy in my life as a whole. She herself was not happy and I suppose she was trying to find out whether others shared her basic discontent. Faced with that full-frontal question I shifted uneasily in a way that could be regarded as characteristic of the English, and then said "Yes" without thinking about it; or only thinking about it to the extent that if I said "No" I knew I would be involved in talking about myself in a way I did not wish to do. In fact, it wasn't the kind of question I agonized over. I got on with the job and with living. A very healthy attitude some will say. Nevertheless from time to time it is salutary to ask oneself a question as obvious and fundamental as that; and for some people the subject is inescapable, for they feel the shadow of their own unhappiness.

In recent decades an assumption has grown up that our own happiness is not a proper Christian concern. It is felt that to bother about one's own happiness is self-centred and "selfish". Furthermore, the word *happiness* has come to carry overtones of the trivial and ephemeral. Christianity, it is asserted, is concerned with something else, with duty and obedience. However, in one way or another, we are all seeking happiness and that is how God made us. If God has created us with this great longing for happiness it would be odd if happiness was something he did not want us to think about or seek. In fact, God wants our happiness; it is what he made us for. Human parents want their children to be happy. They tend to know instinctively when they are miserable, and are distressed about it. If this is so of our flawed human love how much more is it true of the divine love. God longs for our happiness even more than we long for it ourselves. If God longs for our happiness and he has created us with a longing for it, it seems churlish, to say the least, not to give some thought to our most deep-seated desires.

The word *happiness* has disadvantages for it suggests a mood that is bubbly and evanescent, rather than solid and enduring. Nevertheless, there are good reasons for using it. Some other obvious words have become so associated with religion that they don't seem to relate to what the ordinary person understands by and seeks for in the way of happiness. The caricature Anglican vicar talking about "joy" with a square jaw and sonorous voice is the obvious example. In fact our ordinary understanding of happiness and what the Christian religion offers are much closer than some people think. In the Sermon on the Mount we are familiar with the translation "Blessed are . . .", but the Jerusalem Bible uses the words "happy" all the way through. "Happy the pure in heart: they shall see God." So does the J.B. Phillips version. This translation, though not necessarily to be preferred in all respects, has a directness and simplicity that immediately relates what our Lord is saying to man's most fundamental search. In St Thomas Aquinas "happiness" translates the Latin word *beatitudo*, a word which is of course related to beatitude and the beatific vision. In the end the Christian understanding of happiness goes beyond ordinary human notions and it is this that words like "joy" and "blessedness" are trying to convey. Nevertheless the reality that these words convey is related to, and fulfils, our deep longing for happiness.

No doubt there are as many visions of happiness as there are people. It is not a bad exercise to imagine what, if you were given health and only twenty-four hours to live, you would spend your time doing. Given the proviso that your house was in order (both your human affairs and your soul) and God had offered you these hours specifically to enjoy some human happiness for the last time, how would you spend your day? Working or playing? With people or alone? The great Dr Johnson said that if he "had no duties and no reference to futurity he would spend his life in driving briskly in a post chaise with a pretty woman." With only a change in the form of conveyance this would still correspond to many a young man's dream of happiness: but it would not, thank God, be everyone's. Yet although the form which happiness takes for different people is endlessly varied we can all agree in rejecting artificial jollity. There is a kind of forced cheerfulness, a relentless looking on the bright side of things, that immediately rouses our suspicions. In Samuel Beckett's play *Happy Days* the central character is a middle-aged lady called Winnie. In the first half she is in the centre of the stage with a pile of sand up to her waist. In the second half she is buried in the sand up to her neck. She spends the play in a monologue of bright sayings, snatches from hymns and prayers trying to keep her spirits up. There is pathos and compassion in the portrayal. But the total effect is literally appalling. We recognize our human situation and the devices we use to stave off awareness of our plight, our mortality and emptiness. No one wants the happiness of Beckett's *Happy Days*. Even the least brave and perceptive of us recognizes that no happiness is worth having unless it has first faced up to the horrors without and the bleakness within. Otherwise our attempts at happiness are simply a cover-up; a desperate compensation. Monica Furlong puts it well:

But am I happy? Sometimes yes and sometimes no. One of the things which middle age has meant for me (and, I suspect, for many, many people) is the uncovering of a fundamental grief and despair for which the energy and enthusiasm of youth acted most effectively as an anaesthetic or at least a denial. If I could just get the circumstances right . . . (so ran the belief of youth), then I could start to be happy.

Maturity, at least for me, seems to lie in the discovery that happiness and circumstances don't have all that much to do with each other; that happiness is more a matter of direction, choice and habit than we suppose, and less dependent upon the accident of circumstances. For me, too, it seems to be allied with giving the fundamental grief and despair space, room and expression, using them as a kind of necessary ballast but not taking so much of them on board that they swamp the vessel.[1]

There can be no happiness where there is pretence, so we have to look at, and be aware of, those bits of us we find distasteful or unpleasant. For most of us this does not mean coming to terms with anything very extraordinary. We are not all characters from a play by the Marquis de Sade. Yet it may mean coming to terms with our very ordinariness, our cowardice, our sense that we have not done much with our lives, our potential emptiness. We may indeed have to face the fact that we have little appetite or courage for life. Yet if we come to terms with all this we will be on the way to happiness; a meagre ration perhaps, but our own; and if we do not go through that process, whatever else we find, it will not be happiness. It may even pass for a time as religion; as cheerful, positive, clap-handy religion: but it will not be that deeper happiness that God has in mind for us.

There are many kinds of happiness. One of the most

enviable is a quiet happiness; the kind of happiness that is there below the surface in a tranquil, ordered and fulfilled life. It is conveyed particularly well in Susan Hill's novel *In the Springtime of the Year*. The book arises out of the death of a husband and the feelings of the young wife in and through her grief. It also conveys, without any false romanticizing of the past, the happiness of her life before the husband died. In the settled marriage, the steady routine, the ordinary caring, there existed a quiet happiness. Yet, without in any way downgrading this kind of happiness, which will be considered in the last chapter, we also desire the happiness which has an ecstatic quality. The word *ecstatic* is used in Paul Tillich's sense to indicate being taken out of ourselves. Although it is a word that is easy to ridicule, and though it is often used to indicate mere enthusiasm, it points to an experience of self-transcendence; a self-transcendence involving the whole being, emotions as well as mind and will, which accompanies our highest moments. A woman once said to me, "I am content. But I'm not happy." I knew what she meant. She was living on her own, sensibly. She had friends and her life was generally in order. The missing element was that she had no experience of being totally taken out of herself, as happens for example when people first fall in love. Contentment is a high achievement. Yet the human spirit hankers after something more. The American poet Wallace Stevens suggests this in his line: "But in contentment I still feel the need of some imperishable bliss."[2] People most usually find this bliss in music or falling in love. Sometimes they find it in nature when the sheer beauty of some scene overwhelms and exalts them. Mystics find it in prayer. We ought all to be able to find it, more often than we do, in worship. The Book of Revelation describes the worship of heaven in these words:

And whenever the living creature gives glory and honour

and thanks to him who is seated on the throne, who lives for ever and ever, the twenty-four elders fall down before him who is seated on the throne and worship him who lives for ever and ever; they cast their crowns before the throne, singing,

> "Worthy art thou, our Lord and God,
> to receive glory and honour and power,
> For thou didst create all things,
> and by thy will they existed and were created."[3]

In this worship the elders fall down and cast their crowns before the throne. It is an image of abandonment, of letting go, of being totally taken out of ourselves in an act of utter adoration.

We want bliss and we want imperishable bliss. St Thomas Aquinas, in his discussion of happiness, argues that in this life our experience of happiness is fragmentary and fleeting. No one would disagree with him. Our final happiness must lie beyond space and time in what lasts for ever. "There can be no complete and final happiness for us save in the vision of God", wrote Aquinas.[4] This happiness, he said, is to be pictured in terms of contemplation rather than activity. "Man's mind is his highest power, and its highest object is divine good; an object for its *seeing*, not for its doing something in practice."[5] God has made us for happiness and our happiness is in him. For he is the source and standard of all that brings us true and lasting pleasure. All insights into truth, all glimpses of beauty, all experiences of love have their origin and unimaginable perfection in him. If we saw him as he is we would literally be in ecstasy – that is, we would be taken out of ourselves in a total adoration that our earthly experience can only hint at.

This emphasis on contemplation, and on the mind being man's highest power, might depress those who are happiest when working with their hands. There are many people, perhaps the majority of us, who do not naturally enjoy reflecting or reading books, but who derive their satisfaction from cooking or carpentry, from gardening or physical exercise. The contrast between contemplation and activity, however, is not as sharp as we suppose. A person who loves woodwork, and who is making a shelf for the kitchen, will probably make it in a contemplative mood. His (or her) activity will not be aggressive or frantic. Hands will be passed over the wood, the grain inspected, the sawing will be rhythmical. In other words, mind and spirit will be at one with the activity and the whole action will be performed with a sense of peace as well as purpose. On the other hand, when we liken the contemplation of God to looking at a landscape or picture, as though what we looked at was static, this is not the whole truth. For God is ceaselessly at work as well as being "the still centre of the turning world".

Loving God involves not only looking at him but being at one with his will and sharing in his work. Perhaps a better analogy than looking at a landscape is painting one. For then there is both the concerted effort to see, the sustained act of attention and appreciation, together with the attempt to embody this in terms of paint and canvas. The seeing and the painting are closely intertwined. This is not meant to downgrade the notion of contemplation, but to widen it. Those who are activist by nature, people who prefer to do rather than look, may have more aptitude for contemplation than they have allowed themselves to believe.

Contemplation involves looking to God himself; gazing upon him and delighting in him for his own sake. This can be a richer form of prayer than meditation, as being with a person and enjoying them is more satisfying than simply thinking about them. Christian meditation means making use of the mind and the imagination to think about God, to understand him better and to draw closer to him. In contemplation we leave aside thinking about God in order to look to him with a loving heart. For a few spiritual writers, notably St Teresa, contemplation seems to be reserved for a few mystic souls at the height of their experience; and no doubt there is a form of contemplation that is way beyond most of us. Nevertheless, the majority of Christian spiritual writers, including St John of the Cross, stress that contemplation belongs to the ordinary Christian life. It is possible only through the action of divine grace in our souls, of course, nevertheless it is a kind of prayer which every Christian believer can expect to practise. The essence of it is a loving, attentive heart directed towards God for himself; being . . . and looking to him with longing for his own sake. This may be wordless or, more likely, it will involve just a few words, as for example when a person says "O God, thou art my God"[6] and then tries to remain in that attentive longing, using a mixture of silence and repetition of the phrase.

God has made us for happiness. Our happiness comes from him: our happiness is found in him: he is our happiness. So our search for happiness is on the right path when we turn our heart with loving attention to God himself.

Happiness and Joy

God is our happiness: yet this, it must be admitted, is too rarified for most of us most of the time. We wonder, when we are being honest, whether this *really* brings happiness. If we are lucky we will have known at least a few moments of human happiness; as a child, in love, through friendship, in music. These moments come upon us unawares: as Wordsworth and C.S. Lewis suggested, we are *surprised* by joy. Yet when these spasms of delight come they seem so much more life-enhancing, so much more the real thing, than our average experience of prayer. How is this fleeting emotion of happiness related to our life in Christ?

First, it is important to recognize that experiences of delight, involving as they do our emotions, are related to our personal psychology. Some people are temperamentally mildly depressed and they experience very few moments of "lift" in their life. Others are by temperament manic-depressive and are capable of great elation and severe depression. Secondly, there are cultural as well as psychological factors present. When I was on the staff of Wells Theological College, an older student came to train for the priesthood. He had spent the whole of his life working in Malawi and was going to return there at the end of his training. Whenever this person, Jim, was with a group, conversation and cheerfulness flowed. There was effervescent contact and communication. I am sure that Jim was by nature a cheerful person, but more significantly he had spent his life with people for whom it was natural to relate rather than withdraw; who were extrovert rather than introvert. This had rubbed off on Jim and in turn it rubbed off on the college community. People usually exaggerate the importance of national characteristics. Nevertheless there are some real differences between races and nations. The English talk about Nordic gloom; but in turn English life seems very gloomy compared, for example, with a black South African church congregation.

There is a given element in our capacity to experience emotional happiness. There is a limit to what we can do in the way of altering our psychological or cultural endowment. This is in no way to belittle emotional happiness. It matters to God as part of our total happiness. Nevertheless, we cannot command emotional happiness. We have been shaped by, and are constrained by, forces outside our control. The perspective on happiness provided by the Christian faith, however, makes a major difference in several ways.

First, because our deepest and most enduring happiness comes in relation to God himself, it directs us to him. This stops us trying artificially to manufacture or prolong the emotion of happiness. It is a commonplace that if we try too hard for something, it is likely to elude our grasp. At the sexual level, if someone is worried that they are not going to experience pleasure and they try too hard to do so, the very act of trying is likely to frustrate the attempt. Pleasure comes as a result of the total act of loving. So with happiness as a whole. If our hope is in God this leaves the appropriate space for emotional happiness, if it is going to come, to come.

Secondly, the Christian faith gives us the conviction, through the death and resurrection of Christ, that one day the sun of happiness will rise and never set. It is possible to have a deep optimism about life, that despite the tragic dimension, the values we cherish will shine out triumphant; that the purposes of divine love will prevail. This gives us the freedom to receive ordinary human happiness, when it comes, without desperately pursuing it at all costs. Again, as Monica Furlong has written:

> Among the many other things that Easter means to the Christian it must also mean a particular sense of proportion about our griefs and sufferings. They hurt, sometimes excruciatingly, but, on the deepest level of all, it is somehow "all right"; and, out of the praise and gratitude and joy that spring from it when we can grasp it, I think that we may give ourselves permission for the more mundane, but wonderfully healing emotion of happiness.[7]

We can give ourselves permission to receive the emotion of happiness, when it comes, with freedom and gratitude all because it is rooted in a happiness that is deep and enduring. In the Bible this profound, lasting happiness is indicated by the word *joy*. It is a word which suggests the ecstatic delight which, it has been suggested in this chapter, is an aspect of that perfect happiness which we seek.

The first and fundamental fact about joy is that it is present in heaven; there is joy in God himself. In one of his parables Jesus likened the Kingdom of God to a woman looking for a lost coin, who when she finds it calls her friends to rejoice with her. "Just so, I tell you, there is joy before the angels of God over one sinner who repents."[8] In order to avoid referring to the divine name Jews sometimes used the euphemism of angels – it is God himself that is referred to here. There is joy not only in the company of heaven but in God himself. Similarly in the parable of the talents, the two people who have put their talents to good use are told, "Enter into the joy of your master".[9]

Secondly, this joy of God is made manifest in Christ who came to share it with us. This emerges particularly clearly in St John's Gospel. Early in the book John the Baptist discusses his relationship to Christ. He likens Christ to the bridegroom and says that he himself is the friend of the bridegroom who "rejoices greatly at the bridegroom's voice; therefore this joy of mine is now full".[10] He is joyful because of Christ, because of his coming and his presence with us. It is a joy in him, for his own sake. In the fifteenth chapter Christ tells his disciples that he is the Vine and we are the branches. So, "Abide in me, and I in you". This abiding is brought about by dwelling in love. "As the Father has loved me, so have I loved you; abide in my love." Then Christ says, "These things I have spoken to you, that my joy may be in you, and that your joy may be full".[11] This joy we are to receive is the joy of Christ himself "that *my* joy may be in you". It is linked with hearing and taking deep into our souls his words about abiding and loving.

When we grasp and respond to these words, Christ's joy dwells in us to overflowing. The joy of Christ comes from hearing and living out the truth of "abiding" and mutual indwelling. Christ dwells in us because of his love for us. He knows us better than we know ourselves. He wants our well-being, our true good, more ardently than we do ourselves. Through his love he is closer to us than our own breathing. He is our fount, our centre, our soul's soul. And we, by a simple movement of the heart, can dwell in him. When we turn in love to him who is so close to us; when we turn in love to others to whom he is so close, we dwell in him who dwells in us. Therein lies our joy.

Thirdly, this is a joy that nothing can destroy. In mysterious words Christ tells his disciples that soon they will not see him and soon they will see him again, words which refer to his death and resurrection, which in John is inseparably linked to the Ascension and coming of the Holy Spirit. "You will be sorrowful, but your sorrow will turn into joy."[12] As after the pain of labour a mother is filled with delight at the sight of her new born child, so "I will see you again and your hearts will rejoice, and no one will take your joy from you".[13]

The joy of Christ is the joy of his resurrection and continuing presence with us. This is a joy which no one can take away from us, for nothing, not even death, can separate us from Christ's love for us. Whatever anyone does to us they cannot destroy our joy, for it comes from our union with Christ, which is unbreakable. We fail but he never fails us. We turn away from him but he does not turn away from us. He remains with us and abides in us. Whatever we are feeling, however dejected or rebellious, this joy dwells within us; neglected, covered over, besmirched, but there, treasure beyond all price to be had for the asking. All we need in order to claim the treasure is to turn to him who has never left us. No one can take that treasure, that joy of Christ, from us, not even we ourselves.

What we have in John's Gospel are not so much the actual

words of Jesus himself, though we may indeed have these, but Christian meditation on the total Christian experience. The Fourth Gospel was written out of the experience of a community of Christian believers which knew life, true life, eternal life, that is, Christ's presence with them, and his joy which nothing can destroy. Similarly when St Paul talks about joy, he clearly sees it as an aspect or expression of life in the Holy Spirit. When dealing with the dispute about whether or not certain kinds of food should be eaten he says, "For the Kingdom of God does not mean food and drink but righteousness and peace and joy in the Holy Spirit."[14] Joy is a facet of our new being in Christ. Like righteousness and peace it arises out of life in the Holy Spirit. It is not a quality we can achieve just by trying, it is the gift of God himself. "May the God of hope fill you with all joy and peace in believing."[15] This is most explicit in the famous list of the fruits of the Spirit. "The fruit of the Spirit is love, joy, peace . . ."[16] Joy is a supernatural quality, a gift from God, arising out of our life in Christ and the Spirit.

Joy arises out of our relationship to Christ and our life in him. This joy frees us to receive the fleeting emotion of happiness with gratitude, but how much of that emotion we are given varies greatly according to temperament. William Wilberforce was by nature a buoyant personality. Everyone who knew him remarked on his exuberance, his sense of fun, his humour. This naturally cheerful disposition may have been helped by the few grains of opium he took every day, for medicinal purposes, but the happy disposition was his from the start. There is an amusing description of Wilberforce at family prayers:

The scene at prayers is a most curious one. William waving his arms about and occasionally pulling the leaves of the geraniums and smelling them, singing out louder and louder in a tone of hilarity! Trust Him, praise Him, trust

Him, praise Him ever more! Sometimes he exclaims "Astonishing! How very affecting! Only think of Abraham, a fine old man, just a kind of man one should pull one's hat to, with long grey hairs and looking like an old aloe."[17]

William Cowper, the poet and hymn writer, belonged to the same religious tradition as Wilberforce, for both had been influenced by the Evangelical revival. Temperamentally, however, he could not have been more different. Cowper suffered from a crippling depression to the extent that though deeply religious and a converted Evangelical he believed himself to be damned. The one human happiness that Cowper found in his life was in small natural objects, plants, flowers, birds and hares. These drew him out of himself and enabled him to leave the gloomy haunts of sadness for a few hours.

Wilberforce and Cowper, of such different temperaments, yet both rooted in something beyond themselves: the joy of Christ, imperfectly experienced now, but one day to be fully known.

In a long poem called *Night Thoughts* C. H. Sisson lies awake at night imagining childhood scenes, then he becomes aware of himself and his cowardice. Finally he relates how he has found happiness in the natural world about him:

> I feed upon
> The natural benefits of leaf and sky
> And fruits in season, when the mind escapes.
>
> Peace be with all men, and all women too,
> Although I have turned back to homely ways,
> Doing what must be done because it must,
> A public world of green and lavish days.

34

For I cannot excuse, no more than reason
A will that breaks the surface of the time:
Fruit comes when fruit will come and that is all
And so I give away even my wishes

Or would do so, if I were perfect here
As once commanded to be perfect there.
Happiness seeks no answer but itself:
Therefore the earth, therefore the sky are mine.[18]

We cannot order up the emotion of happiness when we want it. Happiness, like fruit, "comes when fruit will come and that is all". What we can do is try to root our happiness in the joy of Christ, as a tree roots itself in the soil.

Joy and Suffering

For anyone who is sensitive there is a fundamental problem about the pursuit of happiness, whether it is thought of as a fleeting emotion or as that deep and enduring quality which Christians call joy. How can we bear to be happy when there is so much suffering in the world? This question points to a crucial feature of Christian happiness – it is an anticipation of an ultimate joy that will be shared by "all those who are to be saved", to use Julian of Norwich's deliberately open-ended and inclusive phrase. Joy in the Old Testament is an eschatological concept, that is, it is a quality that belongs to the new age which God will one day bring about. Through the death and resurrection of Christ that new age has dawned but it is not yet here in its fullness; so Christian joy is an anticipation of that final state of total liberation.

In his book *Theology and Joy* Jürgen Moltmann criticizes the fact that so much of our thinking is done in terms of means and ends. We are always doing something in order to achieve or master something. But in Christian thought there is love and joy in God for its own sake; he is an end in himself. Furthermore, he has created us for our own sake. There is a sense in which creation can be regarded as an act of play and its end mutual delight between God and man. So when there is genuine happiness, when someone is delighted in someone for their own sake, or something is appreciated for its own sake, there is an anticipation of the joy of heaven. Furthermore, and this is one of Moltmann's main themes, this happiness is liberating. It breaks the mould of achievement-orientated, domination-based, culture which is the norm both in the West and in Marxist societies. It is delighted play, an anticipation of the delighted play of heaven, which is both real and liberating. So happiness is not an escape from the burden of the world, not a failure of sensitivity. It exists, by God's grace, as a sign of what will be and it helps to bring about what will be. Moltmann reminds us that in the days of Protestant Orthodoxy Easter sermons used to begin with a joke. The cross of Christ "makes possible the new game of freedom. He suffered that we might laugh again."[19]

It is proper that Christians should feel a temptation to be in permanent mourning for the sin and sorrow of the world. It is not inappropriate that at times in its history the Church has thought that sackcloth and ashes are the only fitting garments for those who know they live in a fallen world. For we do live in a fallen world. At every moment people are screaming in agony because of some human neglect or cruelty. Yet it is clear from the gospels that even in the midst of this Jesus was able to enjoy the happiness afforded by human conviviality. "The Son of man has come eating and drinking; and you say, 'Behold, a glutton and a drunkard, a friend of tax collectors and sinners!'"[20] And when critics compared the followers of Jesus unfavourably with the followers of John, who fasted, Jesus replied: "Can you make wedding guests fast while the bridegroom is with them?"[21]

In Jesus the happiness that people in the Old Testament longed for, the happiness that comes with the reign of God in human affairs, has arrived. There is a decisive sense in which through the death and resurrection of Christ the Kingdom of God has already come. This means, as was brought out in the study of joy in John and Paul, that we can already enjoy the fruits of the new age, among them, joy. This joy, though it is not now shared by everyone, is a foretaste of the joy that will come when God is all in all. So, as Metropolitan Anthony of Sourozh has put it:

> If you are really aware of things, of how tragic life is, then there is restraint in your enjoyment. Joy is another thing. One can possess a great sense of inner joy and elation, but enjoying the outer aspects of life with the awareness of so many people suffering and so on, is something which I find difficult.[22]

This joy, although it arises out of our life in Christ, is not unrelated to ordinary human happiness. This joy frees us to receive all moments of human delight and enhances them.

We may give ourselves permission for the emotion of happiness. In Ingmar Bergman's film *Fanny and Alexander*, a film which Bergman has said is his definitive statement about life and art, there is a theatre director much prone to making speeches and generally agonizing over the problems of life. The film is a harrowing one and there is much to agonize over: but at the end, in a speech to his assembled family and friends, the director says suddenly, "Let us be happy when we are happy". It sounds a slight enough statement to have come from so much groping and anguish, yet it is significant not simply for the plot of the film or Bergman's own situation, but for us all. It implies, first, that we do have times of happiness and, secondly, that we should allow ourselves to experience them as such. For if there is a propensity in some people to ignore the unpleasant side of life there is a no less unhealthy tendency in others to see a maggot in every apple of happiness. It is true that every time we are happy, drinking wine with friends, making love, walking in the country, stroking the cat on our lap, there are people in the world screaming in agony, starving and being tortured. There is no way round this fact and it might be thought that the proper Christian attitude, every time we felt relaxed or carefree, was to remind oneself that someone, somewhere, was in anguish. Yet this is not the Christian attitude.

First, if we were all unremittingly aware of all the suffering in the world, life would be agony for all of us for all of the time, instead of for all of us some of the time. It is difficult to think that a loving God would want this; want, that is, all his creatures to be in unrelieved agony. Secondly, without some genuine experiences of emotional happiness it is difficult to see how we could come to know God to be the unsurpassed delight that he is. It is our moments of human happiness that give us a clue to those good things which pass our understanding that God has in mind for those who love him. Thirdly, those who immediately inject a note of gloom into a happy occasion are taking away from the happiness of others. It is difficult to see how this can be an act of love. If at a party to celebrate the seventieth birthday of a member of the family someone gets up and feels it is his duty to remind the assembled gathering of their mortality and of the three people in the road who have just died in the seventieth year of their lives, such a speech could be justified on the grounds that people ought to be constantly reminded of how short life is, of the need to make their souls ready, and so on. Yet such a speech, unless very sensitively done, with lightness and humour as well as conviction, would be out of place. There are simple happy occasions, such as a birthday, which are given to us to enjoy as such.

On the basis of our Christian joy we can say that if we refuse to be happy when we are happy, this is not only churlish but it is a denial of faith and hope. It is in effect saying that Christ has not risen, that there will never be a time when "all will be well". Dr Johnson once met someone he had been at university with and they conversed about themselves. This man, a Mr Edwards, said, "You are a philosopher, Dr Johnson. I have tried too in my time to be a philosopher; but I don't know how, cheerfulness was always breaking in."[23] Because our happiness is grounded in Christian joy we can accept this cheerfulness when it breaks in, without guilt and with a sense that it is a pointer to what will ultimately be. When Gerald Manley Hopkins wrote his poem on Spring he said:

> What is all this juice and all this joy?
> A strain of earth's sweet being in the beginning
> In Eden garden.[24]

There are few if any who will not have experienced the joy that breaks through to us through nature. This often carries a scent of a paradise lost, a hint of Eden. Yet on the Christian view of things the new age which the Bible talks about can also be seen as a new creation, an Eden restored. When we are moved to exclaim, "What is all this juice and all this joy?" we are experiencing, and participating in, what will finally be.

Happiness and Contemplation

The emotion of happiness is unpredictable. So what steps can we take in the pursuit of happiness? Our happiness is rooted in God. It comes from him and he is our happiness.

This deep, abiding and ecstatic happiness is the joy of Christ. What we can do therefore is to orientate ourselves more fully towards God and live his life within us. This comes above all through the capacity to attend to God, to wait on him and long for him.

The concept of attention is in our time above all associated with Simone Weil. In her essay on the purpose of academic study she argued that "the development of the faculty of attention forms the real object and almost the sole interest of studies".[25] By attention she did not mean the physical effort children make at school when their teachers tell them to attend, screwing up brows, holding the breath and contracting their muscles. She meant an attitude in which the mind is open, receptive, waiting and ready to be penetrated by the object. The reason why the development of our capacity to attend is so crucial is that it bears fruit in the life of prayer. Indeed in contrast to the prevailing justifications of study, in which it is seen as either a way of preparing us for a job or as "truth for truth's sake", Simone Weil argued that its prime purpose was that it might bear fruit in prayer. For it is above all in prayer that attention comes into its own.

Within the earlier tradition the prayer of attention has been called by various names. St John of the Cross called it "The prayer of loving attention", Poulain, "The prayer of simplicity", and Bossuet, "The prayer of simple regard". St John of the Cross states the essence of it in the words: "The soul must be lovingly intent upon God, as a man who opens his eyes with loving attention."[26]

The essence of this prayer is its simplicity. It is no more or less than learning to say the opening words of Psalm 63, "O God, thou art my God", from ever deeper layers of our being. In this prayer we are taken out of ourselves (which is ecstasy). We are beginning to be captivated by that sublime conjunction of beauty, truth and goodness, which is the divine glory; in short, we are beginning to discover the joy of God himself. In the light of this joy all things are seen in their proper perspective and we are set free to experience the healing emotion of happiness as a welcome gift. This emotion of happiness is a notorious will-o'-the-wisp. He comes: he goes. We cannot command him to come: and though we cling to him and plead with him to stay he strides out of the front door of our lives with no word about when, if ever, he might be back.

When happiness comes it is marvellous to have him with us. He smiles and laughs and delights our whole being. But he is essentially a visitant, a messenger, an angel. His presence brings us a foretaste of that ultimate state of affairs when God will be all in all. But that God we do have now, at all times and in all circumstances. The happiness we long for, a happiness of surpassing delight, endlessly sustained, lies in God himself. The way to be happy is to know God better; to live closer to him; to love him more.

✠

O God,
You have set within us a great desire for happiness.
Lead us in the way to find it.

Heavenly Father,
We long for happiness,
but lead us beyond happiness
to that joy from which nothing can take away.

In thy presence is the fullness of joy, and at thy right hand there is pleasure for ever more. (Psalm 16:12)

NOTES

1. *Church Times*, 5 June 1981.
2. Wallace Stevens, "Sunday Morning" in *Selected Poems*, Faber 1965, p. 32.
3. Revelation 4:9–11 (RSV).
4. *Summa Theologica*, 1a, 2ae, 3, 8.
5. ibid, 1a, 2ae, 3, 5.
6. Psalm 63:1.
7. *Church Times*, 15 May 1981.
8. Luke 15:10 (see also verse 7).
9. Matthew 25:21 and 23.
10. John 2:29.
11. John 15:11.
12. John 16:20.
13. John 16:22.
14. Romans 14:17.
15. Romans 15:13.
16. Galatians 5:22.
17. Oliver Warner, *William Wilberforce*, Batsford 1962, p. 155.
18. *PN Review*, 30, p. 18.
19. J. Moltmann, *Theology and Joy*, SCM 1973.
20. Luke 7:34.
21. Luke 5:34.
22. Anthony Bloom, *God and Man*, DLT 1971, p. 16.
23. Boswell's *Life of Johnson*, Everyman 1949, Vol. II, p. 218.
24. "Spring", *The Poems of Gerald Manley Hopkins*, ed. W.H. Gardner and N.H. MacKenzie, OUP 1970, p. 67.
25. *Waiting on God*, Fount Paperbacks, p. 66.
26. See Dom Cuthbert Butler, *Western Mysticism*, 1922.

FOR DISCUSSION

1. Is it true that everyone, in one form or another, is really pursuing happiness?

2. How far does the capacity for happiness depend on temperament?

3. Is joy something different from happiness?

3.

Peace

What Kind of Peace?

I will arise and go now, and go to Innisfree,
And a small cabin build there, of clay and wattles made;
Nine bean rows will I have there, a hive for the honey bee,
And live alone in the bee-loud glade.

And I shall have some peace there, for peace comes
    dropping slow,
Dropping from the veils of the morning to where the
    cricket sings;
There midnight's all a glimmer, and noon a purple glow,
And evening full of the linnet's wings.

I will arise and go now, for always night and day
I hear lake water lapping with low sounds by the shore;
While I stand on the roadway, or on the pavements gray,
I hear it in the deep heart's core.[1]

This poem by W. B. Yeats has had enormous appeal. Apart from its magical, musical qualities, that particular combination of sound and rhythm that make it a poem, there are two reasons for this. First, it puts into words the longing we all share for peace. "And I shall have some peace there, for peace comes dropping slow." Secondly, it envisages this peace reaching us, being imparted to us, through nature.

Sir Kenneth Clark, in a famous television series on civilization, maintained that it was only in the eighteenth century, and in particular through the influence of Jean-

Jacques Rousseau, that European men and women discovered nature. Before then, he argued, mountains had been regarded simply as a nuisance, a barrier to communication. Perhaps Sir Kenneth made the contrast between the eighteenth century and what went before too strong. We need think only of the much loved Coverdale version of Psalm 121, "I will lift up mine eyes unto the hills: from whence cometh my help".

Nevertheless something happened in the eighteenth century and in particular with the Romantic movement that we associate with a poet like Wordsworth. People began to find a religious quality in nature that they were no longer finding in the Church. In the eighteenth century, organized religion tended to be dry, formal and rational. Those feelings of wonder and awe, of the sublime and the numinous, which are associated with religious worship, were for many people aroused not by worship but by nature, especially by mountains and lakes. There is nothing inherently unchristian about this. For we live in a sacramental universe, a world in which matter has been created by God as good, and which can body forth to us something of his reality. "The world is charged with the grandeur of God."[2]

Yet it is a false romanticism that expects nature, of itself, to bring peace of mind; unfortunately it is one we are prone to. We who live in cities, and most of us do, tend to idealize the countryside in a way the true country dweller does not. Caught up in the noise and hassle, the traffic, planes and hurrying rush of crowds, we look at our calendars, with their beautiful pictures of some country scene, and sigh. Or, like Yeats, it is as he stands "on the roadway, or on the pavements gray", that he hears in his heart the lapping of lake water on the shore of Innisfree.

But what about the midges you could reasonably expect to find if you arrived at the lake? Or the irritating people you might find there? Or those you are with who sometimes annoy you? Or your own inner discontents? Nature can be a great balm, and many a person on a long walk through the hills experiences its healing. But it only requires half a moment's thought and a modicum of common sense to know that nature itself cannot bring lasting peace of heart. So people look elsewhere; they look, rightly and reasonably, to religion. If a stranger is seen sitting or kneeling in church on a week-day, it is more than likely that he is seeking some kind of inner peace in a time of anxiety. If a person suddenly starts to come to church, after a gap of many years, it is likely that she has been prompted by an inner dissatisfaction. If on the BBC's *Prayer for the Day* a contributor uses a prayer conveying serenity or tranquillity, hundreds of people will write in asking for a copy. People want peace and they believe there is a close connection between this state of mind and prayer.

Imagine yourself in a scene which normally brings you great delight. Perhaps sitting in the garden reading a book in the sun, or talking to someone you like very much. Then the postman arrives bringing a letter that shatters your calm. It tells you about the illness of someone close to you or it is a hostile letter from someone who gets under your skin. Then a great quarrel starts up next door and you cannot think of anything except the ugly noise. You try to block out the noise and to put the content of the letter out of your mind. But it is difficult, and anyway is this the right thing to do? We are up against the problem and paradox of peace. It seems that what we long for can only be had by shutting out the worry and pain of the world; and to do this feels like a failure of love. If you are worrying about your daughter, who is very ill, you do not have peace of mind. But deliberately to shut out all thought of her illness seems both a denial of love and the road to unreality.

In the trenches of the 1914-18 war, Wilfred Owen let his

mind dwell on those who seemed able to cut themselves off from the carnage about him:

> Happy are men who yet before they are killed
> Can let their veins run cold.
> Whom no compassion fleers . . .
>
> And some cease feeling
> Even themselves or for themselves.
> Dullness best solves
> The tease and doubt of shelling . . .
>
> Happy are these who lose imagination
> They have enough to carry with ammunition
> Their spirit drags no pack.
> Their old wounds, save with cold, can not more ache.[3]

Yet after apparently envying people who are like this Owen turns, in the last verse, and fiercely repudiates them:

> But cursed are dullards whom no cannon stuns,
> That they should be as stones.
> Wretched are they, and mean
> With paucity that never was simplicity.
> By choice they made themselves immune
> To pity and whatever mourns in man
> Before the last sea and the hapless stars;
> Whatever mourns when many leave these shores;
> Whatever shares
> The eternal reciprocity of tears.

Wilfred Owen rejected this kind of "Insensibility", which is the title of the poem. People who choose this way of living sell their human birth right and become stones. Most people would agree with Wilfred Owen. Given the choice between a peace of mind that was attained by making ourselves immune to duty and whatever mourns in man or being flayed by painful experience, we would choose the latter. We choose to remain open and sensitive to what is about us, however ghastly. In so doing we preserve our humanity: but where is the peace?

If we allow ourselves to be aware of the suffering of others then this means we also remain open to the call to alleviate that suffering. This invariably means effort, struggle and perhaps opposition. And these take us even further away from that desirable "peace". So perhaps the peace we long for is not really a legitimate state of mind for a Christian to desire? When Martin Luther King was in prison as a consequence of his work for civil rights in the Southern States of America, he received a letter from twenty white ministers urging him to be more cautious and patient, less ready to stir up trouble. In a famous reply Martin Luther King wrote, "Peace is not the absence of tension but the presence of justice". That understanding of peace is thoroughly biblical. For the biblical word *Shalom* does not refer simply to an inner tranquillity. It means life in all its aspects, outward and material as well as inward and spiritual, in the state of well-being which God intends for it. It certainly includes justice, as well as harmony.

So before taking our longing for peace as authentic, we need to examine what kind of peace it is that we should be seeking. Christians today moralize a great deal on the assumption that peace is an unquestionable good, the highest good. But the Bible in speaking of peace is more often than not warning us against a false peace. People cry "Peace, peace" and the prophets warn them that the kind of peace they want is not available. Christ himself said, "I came not to bring peace but a sword". There is more in the New Testament about the inevitability of division and opposition than there is about peace. That is why I like the prayer used sometimes by the Corrymeela Community in Northern Ireland:

Show us, good Lord, the peace we should seek,
the peace we must give,
the peace we can keep,
the peace we must forego,
and the peace you have given in Jesus Christ our Lord.[4]

The Peace We Can Keep

This prayer says rightly that there is a peace we must forego.
It also suggests that there is a peace we can keep, a peace God
has given us in Jesus Christ. Before exploring the nature of
this peace, however, two further points need to be made
about what this peace is not. First, as was indicated in the
last chapter, we all vary a great deal in our personal make-up
and some people have to cope with a great deal of anxiety and
guilt. For a variety of reasons over which they had no control,
birth traumas, breast feeding difficulties and unsatisfactory
relationships with parents in the first few years, some people
are left with a legacy of worry. Others, on the other hand,
but for reasons over which they also had no control, are
naturally sanguine, placid, even complacent. Often it is the
person with the highest level of anxiety or the one most eaten
into by irrational feelings of guilt who is most desperate to
find peace of mind. Through Christ that person can indeed
find peace and that peace has a healing effect on every aspect
of our personality. Nevertheless, it is likely that they will
always have a residue of inner worry to cope with, as someone
else might have to cope with diabetes or arthritis.

Secondly, it may be that we are meant to have a certain
restlessness about us, which stops us remaining content with
what is finite and limited and which drives us on to
apprehend more of what is infinite and unlimited. George
Herbert wrote a famous poem called "The Pulley", in which

he envisaged God bestowing every gift upon man, except one.

> When God at first made man,
> Having a glasse of blessings standing by,
> "Let us," said He, "poure on him all we can;
> Let the world's riches, which
> dispersed lie,
> Contract into a span."
>
> So strength first made a way;
> Then beautie flow'd, then wisdome,
> honour, pleasure;
> When almost all was out, God made a stay,
> Perceiving that, alone of all his treasure,
> Rest in the bottom lay.
>
> "For if I should," said He,
> "Bestow this jewell also on my creature,
> He would admire my gifts instead of Me,
> And rest in Nature, not the God of nature:
> So both should losers be.
>
> "Let him keep the rest,
> But keep them with repining restlessness.
> Let him be rich and wearie, that at least,
> If goodnesse leade him not, yet wearinesse
> May tosse him to My breast."[5]

God leaves man with a certain restlessness that he might always press on to find his true rest more deeply in God himself.

Although we need to be on the look out for imposters under the name of peace, there is a true peace which Christ himself has promised us:

Peace I leave with you; my peace I give to you; not as the world gives do I give to you. Let not your hearts be troubled, neither let them be afraid.[6]

What is this peace which Christ gives, which is "not as the world gives'? The clue is to be found not only in the context of this saying but in John 20. On the evening of the first Easter the friends of Jesus are together in a small room. Suddenly he is there with them, greeting them with the words "Peace be with you". Then, before he bestows the Holy Spirit on them, again he gives the greeting, "Peace be with you". Finally when eight days later the friends are again together, this time Thomas being with them as well, Christ is once more in their midst with the familiar greeting "Peace be with you".

This greeting, *Shalom*, was of course the usual way people wished one another well but it nowhere else occurs in the Fourth Gospel, and here it is repeated three times in a short space. In this context it is no ordinary greeting and in the mind of the author it clearly refers back to the peace that has been promised in chapter 14. This peace is explicitly related to the resurrection. Verse 28 of chapter 14 reads, "You heard me say to you, 'I go away, and I will come to you.'" The peace of Christ is intimately associated with his resurrection and continuing presence with his Church. Christ's peace is the peace of a union with God which nothing, not even death, can destroy.

D. H. Lawrence began his poem called "Pax" with the line:

All that matters is to be at one with the living God.[7]

This is true and being "at one with the living God" is what Christ was and is on behalf of all of us. In Jesus the Eternal

Son of God became incarnate and under the conditions of finite, sinful human existence he lived a life of unbroken union with the father. In Jesus God and man are joined never to be unjoined; heaven and earth are held together in a union that can never be broken. A Christian is a person who is "in Christ"; that is, through faith and baptism, he is joined to Christ and Christ dwells in him. The images which the New Testament uses to indicate this union, limbs of a body, branches of a tree, indicate a union so close it can only be described in organic terms. This means that what is true of Christ is, through him and in him, true for us also. The union of God and man, of heaven and earth in him, is ours also. We also are joined to our heavenly father with a bond that can never be broken.

This union is already, and always, ours as sheer gift. Despite the Reformation emphasis on our salvation being a gift from God, rather than a reward which we have to earn, all forms of Christianity, Protestant as well as Catholic, find it difficult to receive what is given us. There is a bit of us which always feels it must merit salvation. But whatever the circumstances we are in, whatever our state of mind or feeling, the reality is that in Christ, through his death and resurrection, God and man are one; and we are one with Christ.

Some mystics have talked about the "prayer of union" as the pinnacle of the life of prayer. Without denying the validity and value of this experience such prayer is the appropriation of what belongs to all Christians by virtue of their Christian faith. "The prayer of union" is not something to be achieved by our own striving, but is a working out at a deeper level of what in Christ has already been given to us. How can this prayer of union become more of a reality for all of us?

One of the most precious moments for all Christians occurs at the Eucharist when a person receives Holy

Communion. This is a moment of holy union, a holy communion. It is a moment when the reality of the Christian life, our union with God in Christ, is sacramentally renewed. But how far is this sublime moment allowed to persist and permeate the rest of the day or week? It would be good if we could relive that Holy Communion in our hearts, and rest quietly in it during the day. That holy union, like our incorporation into Christ, is an objective reality. All that is required of us is that we bring it to mind and allow our souls to slip into its abiding serenity.

This union with God does not depend on our own efforts. It is an indestructible reality because Christ, who is one with his heavenly father, is with us and within us. Nevertheless we can take steps to make this reality and the peace it imparts more truly part of us. We can so apprehend this reality that it does not simply sit at the top of our mind as a nice idea but becomes part of our very being. The medium, or environment, through which we can do this is silence.

Silence and Stillness

Most of us find it difficult to use silence well. Our minds wander all over the place and unless we are careful we simply create a vacuum in the mind in which all kinds of unwanted fears and spites come in. Yet it is above all in silence that life can begin to take on depth. In *The Screwtape Letters* C. S. Lewis pictures a devil banishing both music and silence from the world and filling it instead with noise, "Noise which alone defends us from silly qualms, despairing scruples, and impossible desires. We will make the whole universe a noise in the end."[8] It is no accident that in places of Christian renewal, such as Taizé, there is a great emphasis on silence. The difficulty, if we are not at a place like Taizé or on retreat, is to find any in the bustle and noise of the modern world.

Heinrich Boll, the German novelist, has a story about a man who works in a broadcasting station. His name is Murke. He's asked what he keeps in a certain biscuit tin next to his desk:

Murke coloured. "It's – " he stammered, "I collect a certain kind of left-overs."

"What kind of left-overs?" asked Mumkoke.

"Silences," said Murke, "I collect silences." Mumkoke raised his eyebrows, and Murke went on:

"When I have to cut tapes, in the places where the speakers sometimes pause for a moment – or sigh, or take a breath, or there is absolute silence – I don't throw that away, I collect it . . .

"I splice it together and play back the tape when I'm at home in the evening. There's not much yet, I only have three minutes so far – but then people aren't silent very often."[9]

One night Murke is sitting at home with a pretty blonde. Between them is a tape recorder recording – not a word was spoken, not a sound made.

"I can't stand it," said the girl suddenly, "I can't stand it, it's inhuman, what you want me to do. There are some men who expect a girl to do immoral things, but it seems to me that what you are asking me to do is even more immoral than the things other men expect a girl to do."

Murke sighed. "O hell," he said, "Rina dear, now I've got to cut all that out; do be sensible, be a good girl and put just five more minutes' silence on the tape."

"O Rina," he said, "if you only knew how precious your silence is to me. In the evening, when I'm tired, when I'm sitting here alone, I play back your silence."[10]

A desperate measure. Yet it brings out the point that if we want silence in the modern world we will have to take some definite step to find it.

Silence is no negative thing. We talk about a hostile silence or a cosy silence. We invest silence with particular qualities. Charles de Foucauld wrote in a letter to a friend, "You have been constantly in my thoughts and prayers during this long silence. Silence, you know, is just the opposite to coldness and forgetfulness. It is in silence that we love most ardently." The purpose of silence in prayer is that it might lead us into something highly positive. Gerard Manley Hopkins made the point in a poem:

> Elected silence sing to me
> and beat upon my whorlèd ear
> Pipe me to pastures still
> and be the music that I long to hear.[11]

We elect silence, that is, we make a space for silence in our lives, however short, in order that it might pipe us to pastures still, that it might lead us into an inner stillness. For it is in this stillness that we become aware of God: and it is through becoming more aware of God that we are drawn into a profounder stillness.

There are a number of famous sentences in the Bible that are useful in helping silence lead us into stillness.

> Stand in awe, and sin not:
> commune with your own heart
> in your chamber and be still.[12]

> Hold thee still in the Lord,
> and abide patiently upon him.[13]

54

There are also many other sayings both in poetry, for example in T. S. Eliot, and in other religious traditions, that can be of use. The Indian playwright and poet Tagore once wrote:

> Sit still, my heart, do not raise your dust.
> Let the world find its way to you. [14]

The trouble is that on many occasions the heart will not sit still. It raises a continuous cloud of dust in the form of agitation about this, that and the other. We are full of worries or resentments, and instead of inner calm all is seething.

There are a number of ways in which we can help ourselves in this situation. One is to concentrate on getting our physical state relaxed. If we sit up in a relaxed position, knees together, feet on the floor and with hands open on the knees, palms facing upwards (receptive and ready to receive grace) this is a start. Then we can begin breathing rhythmically, according to our own cycle and without straining; but thinking for a minute or two of the breathing process and nothing but the breathing process. This helps to settle the physical frame. Nor is there anything to be ashamed of about this. We live in a sacramental universe in which the outer is just as important as the inner, and in this case a peaceful body can help prepare the soul to receive peace.

Then, if we have particular problems or feelings on our mind it can help to enter imaginatively into the Gospel story of the stilling of the storm (Mark 4:35–end). This story was a mini-meditation or sermon from the time it was first remembered and re-told. In Mark's Gospel it is particularly directed at the persecuted Christians in Rome. They were in the small boat of salvation, the Church, buffeted by the storms of the world. What was God doing about it? He seemed to be asleep. No, says the story, "The Lord is king, be the people never so unpatient: he sitteth between the cherubim, be the earth never so unquiet." [15] So only have faith, the Lord will calm the forces that batter us. "'Peace, be still.' And the wind ceased, and there was a great calm." Those who like to use their imagination in prayer (which is not everyone) can picture themselves in a boat, with the anxieties which are beating upon their mind as waves. Then Christ stands in our soul and says, "Peace, be still." This method should not be dismissed as a technique, or derided as a piece of self-indoctrination. It is simply a way of apprehending, through the imagination, a spiritual truth.

The purpose of silence is to lead us into stillness and the purpose of stillness is to help us become more aware of God.

Be still then, and know that I am God.[16]

Stillness and awareness are intimately connected. They are connected in two ways, for stillness is both the precondition and the consequence of increased awareness. An example of the latter is when children come across a hedgehog. They stop, tell one another to be quiet, tiptoe closer, bend down and look. There is more in this sequence than the fear of disturbing the hedgehog and sending it scuttling into the undergrowth, though this fear itself implies a form of respect. Rather the hedgehog by its very presence, its sheer reality and distinctive individuality, brings a sense of hush. The children are going along talking, playing and preoccupied with their own concerns when the hedgehog brings them up short and silent. So it can be in relation to God. People record being made aware of his reality "out of the blue" and this awareness has brought an inner peace of mind. Yet, in the nature of the case, this reality cannot be commanded. God makes himself known, or known more deeply, according to his own purposes. So it is the first aspect of the connection between stillness and awareness that must be our main concern; stillness as a precondition for the dawning of God's reality.

When painters sit down before a landscape that they want to depict they first look and see, look and see, look and see. They want what is before them to reveal itself, to make it known as it is in all its sheer, unsuspected, surprising reality. So the painter tries, as far as possible, to empty the mind of other thoughts, preconceptions, clichés of art, in order that the reality before the eyes may dawn as it is. In our relation to God this is of particular importance, for inevitably we project onto God our own hopes and fear. To some extent we cannot help creating him in our own image as a god we most want or most fear. Stillness in the soul better enables God to make himself known to us as he is, more in his terms and less in ours. That is why in some famous lines in *The Four Quartets*, which derive from St John of the Cross, T. S. Eliot writes:

I said to my soul, be still, and wait without hope.[17]

Then he goes on to say that we are to wait without love and faith and thought as well. We always invest the object of our hoping, loving, believing and thinking with all too human characteristics, reflecting our own limitations. Yet, of course, as Eliot goes on to suggest, the faith and love and hope are all there, in the very act of waiting upon God: in the stillness.

This stillness is a preparation for God: it is also a participation in God, for he is himself stillness to a supreme degree. One of the key ideas in the thought of St Augustine is that God is *quies*, rest, or eternal rest. This is the background to the famous prayer that our hearts are restless until they rest in God himself. He is eternal rest, the dynamic stillness at the heart of the universe. *Tua quies tu ipse es*. This means that the stillness which is a preparation for knowing God and the stillness which is God himself interact upon and mutually reinforce one another. Stillness of soul prepares us for God and the dawning of his reality enhances that stillness.

Stillness in Agitation

The stillness we find in a special time of silence with God is there to be carried into the day. During an average day we experience a great variety of moods, some of elation but others of dejection, melancholia, or just sheer tiredness. At some times we tend to think that we ought to be stirring ourselves, if not into action, at least into prayer; but sometimes we have the wrong idea of prayer, thinking of it in terms of straining or forcing. Yet all that is necessary is that we quietly allow ourselves to be aware that, whatever we are feeling and however little effort we can make, Christ is with us and within us. He is there in and through the depression or weariness or plain indifference. We are not asked to force ourselves into anything, simply to rest in that central abiding peace at the core of our being – which is there, whatever we feel – because Christ is there.

The peace which Christ offers does not come by shutting our eyes to the horrors of life; on the contrary, being inseparable from his love, it enables us to be open to those horrors. The peace which Christ offers does not involve a distancing of ourselves from the struggles of mankind for justice, order and peace in the world. On the contrary, it enables us to take our place in the struggle. But it does offer a fundamental inner steadfastness in the midst of the pain and turmoil of the world. We see it in a few people, Mother Teresa of Calcutta, for example, in whom totally dedicated social action and Christian serenity clearly go hand in hand. This peace is derived from the presence of Christ. This is the mystery the Church proclaims. St Paul said, "Christ in you" (Colossians 1:27). This peace, which is not a feeling but a fact, is the unbreakable union of God and man in Christ, a union which in principle has broken down every other barrier that human beings erect. "He is our peace" (Ephesians 2:14). We can know this peace now, as an inward stillness. But this peace of soul is a sign of that ultimate peace which will bind all peoples to God and one another. It is therefore a peace which we carry with us and which enables us both to act peacefully in the conflicts of life and to bring a healing peace to them. Cardinal Hume wrote about his time in a monastery in these words:

> I used to find, and still do so, that if I get worked up, excited about some issue, however trivial, in the school or the monastery, because I am at odds with myself and upset in myself, I seize on this and raise it as a banner. It is easy to do this; it is easy to project my own agonies into other people's situations or find an issue in which I get excited . . . Now, I have found that when I try to get back to a positive approach, in which reflective reading matters, in which I want to like silence, in which I try to be alone at times with God, then the calm returns, and with the calm comes perspective.[18]

What Cardinal Hume describes in this passage are the age-old, tried ways of apprehending the peace of Christ: reflective reading, silence, being alone with God. The peace we find when we do these things can be carried, and is meant to be carried, into the day with us. St Francis once said these words to his followers:

> Although you are travelling, let your words be as humble and devout as in a hermitage or a cell. For wherever we are, or wherever we go, we always take our cell with us; for our brother body is our cell, and our soul is the hermit who lives in it, constantly praying to God and meditating on him. If the soul cannot remain quiet in its cell, then a

cell made with hands is of little value to a religious.[19]

There is, as Wordsworth said, a "central peace, subsisting at the heart of endless agitation".[20]

We need stillness in order to apprehend this central peace, but once found it can be carried with us through the hurly-burly of the day, suffusing all we do.

✠

> All we need, good Lord, is you yourself;
> not words about you, but your very presence.
> In the silence,
> in the stillness,
> Come, Lord, Come.

NOTES

1. *The Oxford Book of English Verse*, ed. Helen Gardiner, OUP 1972, p. 816.
2. Gerard Manley Hopkins, "God's Grandeur" in *Poems*, ed. W. H. Gardner and N. H. Mackenzie, OUP 1971, p. 66.
3. "Insensibility" in *War Poems and Others*, ed. Dominic Hibberd, Chatto and Windus 1975, p. 89.
4. Originally published in *Contemporary Prayers for Public Worship*, ed. Caryl Micklem, SCM 1967, p. 48.
5. George Herbert, "The Pulley", in *A Choice of George Herbert's Verse*, selected by R. S. Thomas, Faber 1967, p.68.
6. John 14:27.
7. D. H. Lawrence, "Pax" in *The Complete Poems*, Vol. II, Heinemann 1972, p. 700.
8. C. S. Lewis, *The Screwtape Letters*, Fount Paperbacks, 1977, p. 114.
9. Heinrich Boll, "Murke's Collected Silences" in *Absent Without Leave*, Weidenfeld and Nicholson, reprinted by Calder and Boyars 1974, p.295.

10. ibid, p. 294.
11. "The Habit of Perfection" in *Poems*, p. 31.
12. Psalm 4:4.
13. Psalm 37:7.
14. Rabindranath Tagore, "Stray Birds", CXC, in *Collected Poems and Plays*, MacMillan 1958, p. 311.
15. Psalm 99:1.
16. Psalm 46:10.
17. *East Coker* III.
18. Basil Hume, *Searching for God*, Hodder 1979, p. 167.
19. Mirror of Perfection, 65.
20. William Wordsworth "The Excursion" in *The Poems*, Vol. II, Penguin 1977, p. 152.

FOR DISCUSSION

1. What is the peace which Christians must forego?

2. Is the peace which Christ gives us identical with the peace of a quiet conscience?

3. Given we are prone to worry and anxiety, how in practice is it possible to develop more inner peace?

4.

Fulfilment

Fulfilment and Vocation

The German novelist Herman Hesse once wrote:

> When a man tries, with the gifts bestowed on him by
> nature, to fulfill himself, he is doing the highest thing he
> can do, the only thing that has any meaning.[1]

In his novels, and in particular in *Narziss and Goldmund*,
Hesse explored and expressed this creed. Narziss and
Goldmund are two monks in a medieval monastery. Narziss
remains in the monastery all his life following the way of
discipline, reason and order. Goldmund leaves the
monastery to walk the path of human experience. He loves
many women, he creates works of art, he is forced to kill in
self-defence, he sees life in all its beauty and horror.
Eventually he finds his way back to the monastery. In the
concluding meditation of the novel Narziss reflects (and this
is presumably the voice of Hesse himself) that the path
Goldmund chose was also a way to God; and that the way of
rationality and discipline was not obviously better than the
way of feeling, experience and creativity. Yet is this creed
Christian? Hesse's statement that fulfilment is the highest
human goal is one that most Christians instinctively react
against. Moreover, the working out of the quest for
fulfilment in Goldmund leads to a way of life and some forms
of behaviour which are contrary to traditional Christian
standards. Yet the concept of fulfilment cannot be dismissed

as totally unchristian for two simple reasons.

First, fulfilment is something that human parents want for their children. If a child has some musical or mathematical ability, caring parents want that child to develop the potential he or she has in those areas. More generally parents want their children to find work which is fulfilling, and a way of living including relationships, perhaps also getting married and having children, which bring fulfilment. If fulfilment is something that human parents, quite properly, want for their children, how much more does God, who is perfect love, want this for us who are his children? Secondly, we have been created in the image of God and part of what this means is that we share in God's creativity; we have a creative potential to fulfil. Rudyard Kipling wrote a poem expressing his picture of heaven:

> And those that were good shall be happy:
>   they shall sit in a golden chair;
> They shall splash at a ten-leagued canvas
>   with brushes of comet's hair.
> They shall find real saints to draw from –
>   Magdalene, Peter and Paul;
> They shall work for an age at a sitting
>   and never be tired at all.
>
> And only the Master shall praise us,
>   and only the Master shall blame;
> And no one shall work for money,
>   and no one shall work for fame,
> But each for the joy of working,
>   and each in his separate star,
> Shall draw the thing as he sees it
>   for the God of Things as They are.[2]

I like this picture, because it depicts everyone as an artist with an intrinsic delight and satisfaction in their work;

finding fulfilment for their creative potential. The creative potential we all share by virtue of the fact that we are made in the image of God need not be thought of exclusively in rarified cultural terms. It is true that a great many people find satisfaction through music or painting, but others express their creativity in such activities as gardening or do-it-yourself around the house. Gardening is by far the largest leisure industry in the country, and although people do jobs about the house to save money, they usually derive much satisfaction from them.

The drive for fulfilment, as an aspect of our happiness, is strong. I think of a woman whose life was rather unsatisfactory and meandering until she had the children she had always longed for. Or a woman who has had two disastrous marriages but still keeps on bravely with her writing career. Yet despite this, and despite the fact that God is working for our fulfilment, fulfilment cannot be regarded as an end in itself in quite the way Hesse believed: for people do not in fact go out to find fulfilment, as such, or if they do they are likely to be disappointed.

People fulfil themselves in the attempt to realize some vision or calling. A sculptor struggles to realize, in stone or wood, something of which he is aware but not yet fully aware. So with a painter and any creative artist. Jesus was a highly creative person and his parables stand as works of art for all time. Furthermore, his life itself was a work of art. The way he reacted to situations and what he said in them have a continually compelling freshness and power. Yet all this was in response to a vision: the vision of the Kingdom of God, the rule of God in human affairs. Jesus had a vocation or calling from God to proclaim the presence of the Kingdom and to make that presence a reality through what he said and did. For this task all his creative potential was harnessed and in the doing of it his creative impulses found their fulfilment.

What is true of artists in general and what was true of Jesus in particular is true of all of us: fulfilment comes through pursuing our vocation, our calling, our destiny.

Some Christians, like Isaiah and Jeremiah in the Bible, have experienced a strong conviction that God has called them to some specific task or job. Mother Teresa of Calcutta was once the headmistress of a girls school in the North of India, a job which she much enjoyed. Then on a train journey something happened to her:

> It was a calling within my vocation. It was a second calling. It was a vocation to give up even Loreto where I was very happy and to go out in the streets to serve the poorest of the poor . . . In 1964 I was going to Darjeeling to make my retreat. It was in that train, I heard the call to give up all and follow him into the slums to serve him among the poorest of the poor.[3]

Not all Christians, perhaps only a small minority, have such a clear call to something definite. A sense that their life has a shape and purpose may only come later, after much struggle. In Evelyn Waugh's novel *Helena*, the heroine is Helena, the mother of the first Roman Emperor to be a Christian, Constantine. According to legend Helena was a British girl who in great old age made her way to Jerusalem, where she discovered the sites connected with Holy Week and in particular the relics of the cross on which Christ was crucified. In the novel Helena reflects:

> Her work was finished. She had done what only the saints succeed in doing; what indeed constitutes their patent of sanctity. She had completely conformed to the will of God. Others a few years back had done their glorious duty in the arena. Hers was a gentler task, merely to gather wood. That was the particular, humble purpose for which she had been created. And now it was done.[4]

"That was the particular, humble purpose for which she had been created." Elsewhere Waugh made this point more generally:

> God wants a different thing from each one of us, laborious or easy, conspicuous or quite private, but something which only we can do and for which we were created.[5]

This is a bold and startling claim. Yet it is not idiosyncratic. Here are some words of Newman (which could perhaps underlie the passage of Waugh), words with which, for all their force and challenge, many other Christians would identify:

> God has created me to do him some definite service. He has committed some work to me which he has not committed to another. I have my mission. I have a part in a great work. I am a link in the chain, a bond of connection between persons. He has not created me for naught. I shall do his work.[6]

The Call to Become Ourselves

This claim that God has something special in mind for each of us is so staggering and yet, if true, so encouraging, that it needs to be tested for reality. When we reflect on the people we know, can we really detect any hint of the fact that there is some special thing for which they have been created, something which they, and only they, can do? People who are likely to appear in a Barbara Pym novel, such as *Quartet in Autumn*, lead such trivial, disappointing, unfulfilled lives it is difficult to have the kind of faith that Evelyn Waugh and Newman had in the particular point and purpose of every individual existence.

Fulfilment

In *Quartet in Autumn*,[7] Edwin, Norman, Letty and Marcia work together in the office of some large organization in London. They do humdrum jobs of so little use to the firm that the whole office is likely to be phased out soon. They have worked together for years but hardly know one another and never meet outside the office. They have their little routines, their stereotyped phrases, their little ways, all endlessly repeated, all utterly predictable. Letty was the only daughter of middle-class parents. She came up to London, never married and has spent her life working in an office and living in bed-sits. She has only one friend, and even the friend casts a shadow because having been married and having had children she points up the failure in Letty's life. Norman is the male equivalent of this with two added disadvantages: he is unattractive physically and has a sarcastic manner. Marcia shares the same disadvantages as the others with some of her own. She is pathologically alone, suspicious of others and beginning to act very oddly. She is saving all the milk bottles at the bottom of her garden, and hoarding a great pile of tins, whilst eating virtually nothing herself. None of these three have any faith. Edwin, who does, is a widower who spends his whole life going to one church service after another.

What possible point or purpose is there in these lives? Is it for such that God has created the universe? Is it for such as Edwin, Norman, Letty and Marcia that God has made the world? Has he struggled with millions and millions of years of evolutionary development in order to produce this as the crown and climax of the whole process? Faith answers Yes. Yet faith can be strengthened by a number of considerations. First, it is unwise to draw too much of a contrast between our own life, or the lives of those that have some glamour to them and the apparently utterly insignificant lives of people like Edwin, Norman, Letty and Marcia. For, in the end, what do any of our lives add up to? There are moments when we all share the feeling of the writer of Ecclesiastes, "Vanity, Vanity, all is vanity". Secondly, and more positively, the most ordinary life can reveal surprising features and even depths. When she died Marcia, who lived alone in a dirty, untended house, left the house to Norman; much to everyone's surprise. Norman and she did not seem to have anything between them. All they did was share a large tin of coffee in the office, on the grounds that it was more economical to buy the large size. Yet something had once passed between them. There was some undeveloped, unexpressed feeling and capacity for love there.

Many of the early poems of R. S. Thomas are about poor Welsh hill farmers stumbling through the clay, in particular one whom he names Prytherch. Thomas describes the lives of these people, in all their harsh detail. Yet he sees qualities there that others don't have:

> Yet this is your prototype, who, season by season
> Against siege of rain and the wind's attrition,
> Preserves his stock, an impregnable fortress
> Not to be stormed even in death's confusion.
> Remember him, then, for he, too, is a winner of wars,
> Enduring like a tree under the curious stars.[8]

And Thomas warns townspeople not to be superior:

> Don't be taken in
> By stinking garments or an aimless grin;
> He also is human, and the same small star,
> That lights you homeward, has inflamed his mind
> With the old hunger, born of his kind.[9]

Thirdly, it is not for so-called great achievements that God made the universe, or for empires or cultural movements. He made it for individual persons, for each unique soul. When we are inclined to compare ourselves unfavourably with others who seem more talented, or nicer or more worthwhile, it is good to remember that the bit of creation that God has given us a direct hand in, the only bit, is oneself and it is oneself, rather than anyone else, that God wants us to be. There is a saying of Rabbi Zusya of Hanipol: "In the coming world they will not ask me: 'Why were you not Moses?' They will ask me 'Why were you not Zusya?'" Each one of us is what Helen Oppenheimer has described as "an irreplaceable centre of minding".[10] We mind what happens, we can be pleased and we can be hurt; and we are irreplaceable. When the flowers in your vase wither you can throw them away and replace them without feeling any loss. But to the people who love you and to you yourself, no one can take your place. It is that irreplaceable centre of minding that God knows and wants you to be. In one of his poems Gerard Manley Hopkins thinks of each of God's creatures being itself:

> Each mortal thing does one thing and the same:
> Selves-goes itself; *myself* it speaks and spells,
> Crying *What I do is me: for that I came.*[11]

There is in each one of us a quirky, interesting, lively point of view on the universe. It is when we are this self that we feel most alive. It is when we try to conform to some alien stereotype that we are dull both for ourselves and for others. One of the most famous of all cartoonists was H. M. Bateman, who made his name in the 1920s for his drawings depicting the man who committed this or that social gaffe. Yet despite big fees and public success Bateman became an unhappy man. He wanted to be a "serious painter". Although a celebrity cartoonist he gave it all up to devote himself in earnest to painting. Alas, he was a flop, and his life began to disintegrate. It is possible to argue that Bateman wanted a new challenge, that he was quite right to pursue something ostensibly more serious, and that he was quite right to do this even though it brought him no happiness. On the other hand it is possible that Bateman had his own unique gifts and that in employing them he was doing what he should have done; that in wanting to be a "serious" painter, he was simply trying to conform to the generally accepted norm of what was worthwhile rather than being himself and using his god-given talents. In his cartoons he put his actual personality, fears and all; for they express the private disquiet that was part of his personality, as well as amused observation.

The poet Philip Larkin much admires the thriller stories of Dick Francis. In a review, after praising many of his books, Larkin expressed a worry that Francis was departing from his own high standards, perhaps because he was trying to write a different kind of book. "The temptation, already hinted at, for Francis to become 'a real novelist' must be very strong. Let us hope he resists it; he is always twenty times more readable than the average Booker entry."[12]

Again, there is no reason why Francis should not aspire to be "a real novelist" and it is good to be stretched beyond our norm. On the other hand it may be that he, like the rest of us, has certain gifts that are uniquely his.

Talk about painters and novelists contrasts strangely with the people who set up the problem, Edwin, Norman, Letty and Marcia, who in Barbara Pym's novel literally seem to have nothing, nothing in the way of a fresh and creative response to life. Has God really given them nothing? There is a famous parable in the Gospels about three people, one of whom was given ten talents, one five and the third only one. The first two put their talents to good use and doubled what they had been given. When the third person was asked to account for his one talent he said:

"Lord, here is your pound, which I kept laid away in a

napkin; for I was afraid of you, because you are a severe man; you take up what you did not lay down, and reap what you did not sow." He said to him, "I will condemn you out of your own mouth, you wicked servant! You knew that I was a severe man, taking up what I did not lay down and reaping what I did not sow? Why then did you not put my money into the bank, and at my coming I should have collected it with interest?"[13]

The master then takes the one pound and gives it to the one who had ten. This parable, though it had a particular meaning within the context of Jesus's ministry, is absolutely true to life as a whole. Life *is* unfair; some are talented and others are not. Moreover those who have much find it relatively easy to make more whilst those who have little find themselves in a downward spiral of deprivation. The temptation, for those who feel they have little in the way of looks, brains or ability, is to do just what the man in the parable did: sulk resentfully, hide what little we do have and do nothing with it. The parable comes as a sharp challenge to us to make what we can of what we have got, however little it seems. The master in the parable took a hard line with the person who stood apart in sulky resentment.

There is no one with less than one talent, for we have our own person, our own being, that irreplaceable centre of minding. Yet which is the real "me"? Is the real me the person I remember running around in shorts interested only in football? Or the person who likes going out to parties? Or the person who loves best of all curling up with a book? We have so many facets to our person and we appear to have changed so much in the course of our lives. Austin Farrer suggested that it is in fidelity, and in particular in fidelity before God, that the abiding core of our personality is disclosed and developed:

Faithfulness, then, is the thing which most forcibly convinces us of personal identity. If we rely on a friend's words, we know that he will not become a different person; for if he did, he might change his mind and let us down. He may become a different person in many ways; he may change his tastes and occupations, many of his opinions; but he will not become a different person in this particular way; not, that is, in respect of his faithfulness to me.

We commonly say that those who have no faithfulness have no character, no constancy of person at all; they seem to hang together by the mere fact of attachment to a single body; that body being destroyed, what is there, what thread of real being, on which God can bestow a share of his own immortal life?[14]

This, however, is worrying. For if the fidelities in our life are the clues to our identity, our personhood, and we are conscious of our infidelity, our wavering purposes, our inconstancy, what becomes of our identity? Do we really exist? Our hope cannot be in ourselves but only in that unending faithfulness, God himself. We are unfaithful but he is faithful: his loving purpose towards us never fails. We forget him but he does not forget us. In relation to him then, and only then, do we find real continuity and therefore true identity for ourselves.

There is an intriguing passage in the book of Revelation:

To him who conquers . . . I will give a white stone, with a new name written on the stone which no one knows except him who receives it.[15]

In the Bible the name of a person is never simply a word, it stands for the whole person. What the verse suggests is that

Christ gives us our real identity. Who we really are is known only to him and to our own heart's core. Our parents give us a name at birth – John, Mary, Simon, Joan. But the name that is truly ours, the person we really are, is only partly known now. There is all that we have it in us to be. There is the person that God has it in mind for us to be; the person he is helping to emerge and develop. This person has a relationship with God that no one else can have in quite the same way. As Anthony Bloom has written:

> This name . . . contains and defines all that we are and all that we are called to be. We can imagine it to be the mysterious word that God uttered in order to call us into being out of nothingness . . . This name which defines us completely and is known only to God and the one who bears it, defines the unique, unprecedented and unparalleled relationship that each of us has with God.[16]

No one has the particular personality, the set of circumstances, the stance on life, that we have. We bring into our relationship with God what no one else can. The nineteenth-century writer George MacDonald, who was such a powerful influence on C. S. Lewis, made the point:

> Not only then has each man his own relation to God, but each man has his special relation to God. He is to God a special being, made after his own fashion, and that of no one else. Hence he can worship God as no man hence can worship him.[17]

Fulfilment and Work

There is a tendency in some people to think of their Christian life in terms of what they do when the working day or the working week is over. They give, often devotedly, of their spare time and energy to the local church and community. This in itself is good. Yet the best hours of the best years of the lives of most people are spent in paid employment. For most of the hours of daylight, for at least five days a week, from the age of about eighteen to sixty-five, people are putting a large part, and sometimes the best part, of themselves into their work. This means that for most people personal fulfilment must have a great deal to do with finding, or failing to find, fulfilment in work. For much of the time we find work a burden. Philip Larkin likens it to a toad squatting on our shoulder:

> Why should I let the toad *work*
> Squat on my life?
> Can't I use my wit as a pitchfork
> And drive the brute off?
>
> Six days of the week it soils
> With its sickening poison –
> Just for paying a few bills!
> That's out of proportion.

The poem goes on to suggest that what stops him having the courage to shout "stuff your pension" is something inside us:

> For something sufficiently toad-like
>   Squats in me, too;
> Its hunkers are heavy as hard luck,
>   And cold as snow.
>
> I don't say, one bodies the other
>   One's spiritual truth;
> But I do say it's hard to lose either.[18]

In another poem, *Toads Revisited*, he describes walking

around the park and seeing all the people who don't work, people who are physically ill or mentally weak:

> All dodging the toad work
> by being stupid or weak.
> Think of being them!
> Hearing the hours chime.

Despite the fact that work is a toad we want to pitchfork off our shoulder, it helps us get through:

> No, give me my in-tray,
> My loaf-haired secretary,
> My shall-I-keep-the-call-in-Sir;
> What else can I answer.
>
> When the lights come on at four
> At the end of another year?
> Give me your arm, old toad;
> Help me down Cemetry Road.[19]

For most human history work for most people has been sheer drudgery on the land, labouring on roads and buildings, or bending beside a conveyor belt. Perhaps there was no alternative. Yet this wage-slavery effectively killed off and still kills off the creative shoots of millions. Karl Marx believed that man was essentially a creative being. What appalled him as much as anything was to see a person reduced to one mechanical function, turning a screw thousands of times a day, or endlessly hacking at a coal face. He likened this to killing a cow for its hide and throwing away all the rest of the animal, as he thought happened in Argentina at that time. He believed that every person had a whole world of creative impulses inside them. In his perfect society he envisaged people working in the morning, hunting in the afternoon and reading in the evening – an ideal which bears a remarkable resemblance to the life of an educated eighteenth-century squire!

What once was impossible is now becoming more likely. Automation and robots, computers and machines of all kinds, are reducing the amount of sheerly mechanical and repetitive work that human beings have to perform. On the other hand, those jobs which are left require increasing degrees of skill. Furthermore a few (far too few) firms such as Volvo seriously try to organize their work in such a way as to maximize the element of personal satisfaction for their employees. If these trends continue it will be possible for an increasing number of people to find fulfilment in their work. This is what God wills. For, even more on the Christian vision of man than the Marxist one, we are creative beings; and our working life is likely to be the main thrust of our life. There, as much as anywhere, we are meant to find an outlet for the creativity with which God has endowed us.

People who feel they have a vocation to some particular job and who find that doing it brings them fulfilment are happy indeed. But what about the people who have never felt a vocation to anything in particular? Or who find themselves in a job (or out of a job) which is mostly frustration? Cordelia in *Brideshead Revisited* had strong feelings about vocation. She explains to Charles Ryder what is meant by the word:

> It means you can be a nun. If you haven't a vocation it's no good however much you want to be; and if you have a vocation you can't get away from it, however much you hate it. Bridey thinks he has a vocation and hasn't. I used to think Sebastian had and hated it – but I don't know now.[20]

This passage thinks of vocation in too narrowly religious terms and it underestimates our human capacity to deny or disobey our vocation. Nevertheless, it points to a fundamental truth, already referred to earlier in the chapter. God does have something in mind for us. And what he has in mind for us does not concern simply the spare part of our day and the left-over part of our life. He is concerned about what matters most to us, and what matters most to many people is their work. What then can be said to those who have never felt a calling to anything in particular but simply done any job they could get in order to earn a living?

First, God may yet have something different in mind. Mother Teresa received a calling within her calling. Helena found her life's work in great old age. The three-career life is more and more the pattern of the future and this opens up the possibility of people having a second or third career, which they experience more definitely as a vocation. There is also Jung's observation that most of his patients were middle-aged men going through a crisis that he judged to be fundamentally spiritual in character. In middle age the neglected inner life, pushed aside by the pressure of career and bringing up a family, asserts itself. This is often the prelude to a different life-style in the second stage of life, one with greater spiritual content and more personal fulfilment.

Secondly, a person may come to see his or her present job as a vocation, even if it was not entered into in that spirit. One of the reasons people are not able to see their job as a vocation is that they have, like Cordelia, a rather limited view of the type of job which qualifies. One of the great contributions of Martin Luther to Christian understanding was his insistence that any job that was necessary for society should be seen as a potential vocation. Before the Reformation there was a tendency to divide Christians up into two classes: Division One Christians with a vocation to be a priest, monk or nun; Division Two Christians with no vocation. Luther showed how a Christian can have a vocation in the secular world. Any job that was necessary for the maintenance and well-being of society, including those which involved coercion, such as the police and the army, could be regarded by a Christian as a duty and vocation.

There are many very ordinary, perhaps rather dull, jobs which are necessary if society is going to function. These jobs, however mundane, are a way of offering service to others in the name of Christ. Some Christians doing an ordinary secular job think that the "Christian" bit is that which involves relationships and in particular helping or converting people through those relationships. But not all jobs involve relationships and it is not only in that aspect that the job is a vocation. The work itself in all aspects is a vocation if the job is to be seen as a vocation at all. It is a way of serving others and it is a way of co-operating in the creative work of God. So long as God wills human life to continue, he wills human society to continue, for there can be no human persons without an organized human community. Furthermore, so long as God wills society to continue he wills those means without which no society can exist, including the minimum necessary use of coercion both within the state and in the states system as a whole, in order to hold lawless anarchy at bay.

God is ceaselessly at work bringing human beings to their proper fulfilment. This is only possible within human society. Christians, and others, who are trying to meet the basic needs of that society are sharing in God's creative work.

Many millions of people today are unemployed. This is maiming, both to those individuals and to society as a whole, for a number of reasons. First, even though a person's basic financial needs might be met through unemployment benefit, such people have no opportunity to advance themselves. Surrounded by desirable goods they have no opportunity to earn enough money to buy those goods. Their freedom of choice and opportunity is severely limited. Secondly, many feel that it is through their jobs that people define themselves. It is not usually long after meeting someone that we ask them what they do. Thirdly, many people want, rightly, to make some contribution to society as a whole, and a job is the most obvious way of doing this.

As society is organized at the moment it is through a paid job that people define themselves, advance their prospects and make a contribution to society as a whole. In short, it is through a job that they come to have a recognized and respected position in the community. This is denied to the unemployed. It goes without saying both that unemployment must be reduced and every effort made by society as a whole to give the unemployed opportunities of creative outlet and development, for example, through continuing education of various kinds. Nevertheless, we have to face the present frustration of so many. Also, the frustration of all those who are doing jobs in which they find little or no personal satisfaction. Where is the fulfilment in all this? At this point the Christian faith suggests that fulfilment is possible even in the midst of our frustrations, for fulfilment is more than emotional satisfaction. On the Christian view it has to do with a creative adherence to the will of God who turns our frustrations into blessings.

Each day presents us with a series of strict limitations and constrictions. Most of the things we do we simply have to do. There is no getting out of them. Furthermore, the process of ageing means that the limitations become ever more severe and the constrictions ever more confining. This theme is dealt with more fully in chapter six where the forces of diminishment are considered. The point here is that work, or lack of work, for all of us, involves some sheer drudgery, much plain slog, boredom, tiredness, frustration, strain, worry and so on. The conditions which bring these emotions should be changed, so far as they can. And we should go on trying to change them even when it seems difficult or almost impossible to do so. Nevertheless, there will always be a residual recalcitrance in things, not least in our work. This is well pictured in Genesis, when Adam is thrown out of the Garden of Eden and told that his work will be toil and sweat (Genesis 3:17-19). Whatever we do to change conditions for the better there will be a basic hardness about our work (or lack of work) and an inescapable element of difficulty and frustration. It is here, just as much as in the more obviously satisfying aspect of work, that the Christian is to find fulfilment. As Cardinal Hume has put it, echoing Christian teaching down the ages:

> If we look at each moment as a point at which we meet God and make it always a moment of love and surrender to his will, then each moment of our lives can and should become one in which we seek and find God. [21]

Fulfilment and the Will of God

Whether we are at work or at home, whether we are in work or out of it, the will of God is the key reality for our fulfilment. For fulfilment is only possible in so far as we are doing the will of God. God is the fount from whom our being flows. In so far as we are not doing his will, we are poisoning the flow at source. In so far as we are doing his will, the water of life and the wine of glory are pouring into our being. The will of God is not something that is alien to our being. It is coterminous with our deepest striving for personal fulfilment. Nor is it something that is imposed upon us. It is what we choose in response to the revelation of God in Christ, the source and standard of all that we regard as good and true and beautiful. In response to the vision of God bodied forth in Christ, we try to make ourselves more and more open, responsive and available to the purpose of divine love. The spirit is well caught by Psalm 40:

Sacrifice, and meat-offering thou wouldest not:
 but mine ears hast thou opened.
Burnt-offerings, and sacrifice for sin,
 hast thou not required: then said I, Lo, I come,
In the volume of the book it is written of me,
 that I should fulfil thy will, O my God:
I am content to do it;
 yea, thy law is within my heart.[22]

We are able to accept the limitations and constrictions that are part of every day, the difficulties and frustrations, because in doing so we can embrace the will of God wherein our fulfilment lies. Because our fulfilment comes about through sinking ourselves in the Divine purpose and only through that, we are able to act creatively in relation to the frustration of life. We can look for fulfilment from them even when there is little or nothing in the way of immediate emotional satisfaction. For our self is still in the process of becoming and that self is being shaped when things go badly as much as when they go well.

Beloved, we are God's children now; it does not yet appear what we shall be, but we know that when he appears we shall be like him, for we shall see him as he is.[23]

This truth was most beautifully expressed by Dietrich Bonhoeffer, in a poem he wrote whilst in prison for his part in the plot against Hitler, called "Who am I?" It begins with how others saw him:

Who am I? They often tell me
I stepped from my cell's confinement
Calmly, cheerfully, firmly,
Like a squire from his country house.

Inside, however, he felt very different:

> Am I then really all that which other men tell of?
> Or am I only what I myself know of myself?
> Restless and longing and sick, like a bird in a cage.

The poem ends up triumphantly:

> Who am I? They mock me, these
> lonely questions of mine.
> Whoever I am, Thou knowest,
> O God, I am thine.[24]

Who we truly are is a mystery known only to God. It does not matter that we cannot answer all the questions about ourselves for "Whoever I am, Thou knowest, O God, I am thine."

Our fulfilment is about our growth into the unique being whom God has it in mind for us to be. This being finds its identity in relation to God and his steady intent of good-will towards us; in seeking and trying to do his will. Even the inevitable constrictions and frustrations of life can be positively embraced, for if they are inevitable we discover in them not only our duty but our joy: God himself.

✠

> O God, show me more of yourself
> and give me the willingness to respond
> wholeheartedly.
>
> O God, help me to be so open to you
> that your purposes may be furthered
> in and through me.

Fulfilment

Grant us, O Lord,
to know that which is worth knowing,
to love that which is worth loving,
and above all to search out
thy most holy will.

O God, open my eyes to know the task
which only I can do
and give me grace to do it.
Be it unto me according to thy word.

NOTES

1. Herman Hesse, *Reflections*, Panther 1979, p. 82.
2. Rudyard Kipling, "When Earth's Last Picture is Painted", in *Selected Verse*, Penguin 1983, p. 98.
3. Malcolm Muggeridge, *Something Beautiful for God*, Fount Paperbacks 1972, p. 85.
4. *Helena*, Chapman and Hall, p. 259.
5. "The Month" 1952, reproduced in a *A Little Order*, a selection from his journalism edited by Donat Gallacher, Eyre Methuen 1977, p. 184.
6. J. H. Newman, *Meditations and Devotions*, I, 2, Burns & Oates 1964, pp. 6f.
7. Barbara Pym, *Quartet in Autumn*, Granada 1982.
8. R. S. Thomas, "A Peasant" in *Song at the Year's Turning*, Rupert Hart Davis, 1955, p. 21.
9. "Affinity" in *Song at the Year's Turning*, p. 25.
10. Helen Oppenheimer, *The Hope of Happiness*, SCM 1983, p. 92.
11. "As Kingfishers catch fire . . ." in *Poems*, p. 90.
12. *The Observer*.
13. Luke 19:20–23.
14. Austin Farrer, *Said or Sung*, Faith Press 1964, p. 160.
15. Revelation 2:17.
16. *God and Man*, Darton Longman & Todd 1971, pp. 88f.
17. *George MacDonald: An Anthology*, ed. C. S. Lewis, Fount 1983, pp. 8f.

18. "Toads" in *The Less Deceived*, Marvell Press 1973, p. 32.
19. "Toads Revisited" in *The Whitsun Weddings*, Faber 1971, p. 18.
20. Evelyn Waugh, *Brideshead Revisited*, Penguin 1962, p. 213.
21. Basil Hume, *Searching for God*, Hodder & Stoughton 1983, p. 53.
22. Psalm 40, 6–8.
23. 1 John 3:2.
24. Dietrich Bonhoeffer, *Letters and Papers from Prison*, Fontana 1959, p. 173.

FOR DISCUSSION

1. Is the idea of personal fulfilment a legitimate Christian goal?

2. What is the weakness in the twentieth-century stress on personal fulfilment?

3. Is there a distinctly Christian contribution to the understanding of fulfilment?

5.

Success

Ambition for What?

People speak of young men setting out into the world to achieve fame and fortune. Yet this may very well be a fantasy of the middle aged, a projection of their own interest in fame and fortune. Young people are usually interested in more immediate pleasures. In T. S. Eliot's play *Murder in the Cathedral* Thomas Becket says:

> The natural vigour in the venial sin
> Is the way in which our lives begin.
> Thirty years ago, I searched all the ways
> That lead to pleasure, advancement and praise.
> Delight in sense, in learning and in thought,
> Music and philosophy, curiosity,
> The purple bullfinch in the lilac tree,
> The tiltyard skill, the strategy of chess,
> Love in the garden, singing to the instrument,
> Were all things equally desirable.
> Ambition comes when early force is spent
> And when we find no longer all things possible.
> Ambition comes behind and unobservable.[1]

Ambition is a subject about which the English in general and English Christians in particular are generally embarrassed, at least in relation to themselves. Yet we are all ambitious for something and we are right to be. The American lady mentioned earlier once asked me another question. "What are your ambitions?" she said, once again looking me in the eye. I shuffled about in an evasive manner before replying, "I don't think I've got any, actually." "How dull," she retorted. It would indeed be dull if we had no ambitions, indeed we would be dead. In fact, of course, we all do have ambitions, however reluctant we may be to face them ourselves or to talk about them to other people. All of us have ambitions, for whatever success a person might seem to have achieved, it is likely that there will still be goals they have not attained: and these goals will not always be the ones that others suspect.

I was once introduced to a distinguished man who as well as writing large text books did journalistic work. As an intended friendly opener I said, "I've read some of your little pieces in *The Times*". "Little pieces! Little pieces!" he responded. I had assumed that his emotional investment was in his large books. In fact it was just as much in his "little pieces", over which he took a great deal of trouble. Another person I knew had everything that ambition could call for. He owned one of the most famous houses in the country and held one of society's most prestigious jobs. Yet, I suspected that there was an underlying ambition in him not yet fully attained, namely to be well thought of by the artistic community. Those who appear to have everything will almost invariably be found to be wanting something more.

Although Christians are suspicious of ambition it is a God-given part of our nature. No doubt because our nature is flawed it often takes distorted forms, but the basic drive to make something of our lives is not only good but essential. Unless we have some "go" to our personality, some "oomph"; unless we want to leave a ripple, however tiny, on the water of existence, it is difficult to see how we can be said to be alive at all. This desire to make something of our lives, the drive to make a mark, is fundamental and deep-seated. The playwright Samuel Beckett once said, "I couldn't have done it otherwise, gone on I mean. I could not have gone on through the awful wretched mess of life without having left a stain upon the silence."[2] It is part of the dignity and glory, the mystery and pain, of being human, that even when a person feels, as Beckett does, that it is all silence, he still wants to make a stain upon that silence.

People have different ambitions. Some want to make money and it is common in Christian circles to be disparaging about this. Too often this judgement reflects a lack of awareness that our attitude to money can reflect our social situation. Those who have no money know the value of money. Those whose grandfather made money may sit light to it. Grandfather made money, clambering out of the soil or mine to build a business. Son worked at the business and made it better. Grandson discovered more interesting things in life like art or religion; or sadly, less interesting things like drugs. In any case, always used to money, he can become disparaging about it. Those who work for money, particularly those who get paid weekly wages, know its value. It not only buys what is essential. It can, in greater quantities, enlarge the area of freedom. As the great Doctor Johnson said, a man who spoke with robust common sense about money, as he did about most subjects: "It will purchase all the conveniences of life; it will purchase variety of company; it will purchase all sorts of entertainment."[3] He also said: "There are few ways in which a man can be more innocently employed than in getting money."[4]

The great advantage of money transactions, of working for money and buying something for money, is that what is happening is for the most part open. When money is not present, when we are doing kindnesses, or favours, or duties, all sorts of good things may be going on, but there will also be a hidden transaction; there will be emotional satisfactions that not everyone will know of or want to know of. There can be something honest about money. When sometimes I have taken a wedding and the father of the bride, as he has been leaving the vestry after the signing, has slipped a note into my hand with the words, "That's for you, Father", I have been pleased not only by the kind thought but at the straightforwardness of the gesture.

People want money; and those who make money sometimes want more and more. Thomas Traherne did not criticize this, on the contrary he welcomed it as a sign of the insatiable appetite that God has deliberately given us, for it is the will of our heavenly father to give us the universe. The problem, as Traherne saw it, is not that we are greedy but that we are not greedy enough. Yet we can question whether this desire to possess is quite the final goal that Traherne makes it. For what happens when people make a lot of money? They use it not only to buy various forms of pleasure; they often use it to buy a position or a good name. A person who has made a fortune does not want to be known as a person who has made himself rich. He wants to be an honoured and respected member of the community. There are many ways in which money can be used to achieve this. It is no longer possible to buy peerages and knighthoods for a fixed sum, but contributions to political parties, the arts, and good causes of many kinds enable a person to become a respected figure and therefore one worthy of consideration for an honour. There is nothing reprehensible about this. It simply means that money is not the end goal. People use money to purchase other goods, in particular a position in the community.

Is it power that all men seek after? On the contrary, the pursuit of power is a minority interest. Despite the fascination of the media with power, in politics and the boardroom, few people are driven by a lust for power. The simple reason is that power, except in one notorious profession (and it is probably not really power which that profession possesses but influence), always carries responsibility. People in power have to make decisions and making decisions is not easy. It always means excluding certain opinions, certain people or certain interests. In short, it means bearing some opprobrium. Only those who can cope with "aggro", only those who can live with the fact that every decision they make hurts some people as well as helping others, can cope with power. Most people prefer a quieter life; indeed many of those who find themselves in power are looking forward to a quieter life.

It is true that some people long for the fruit of power. Lord Reith, the founder of the BBC, always felt bitter that he had never been asked to do a job that was big enough for him. A deposed Prime Minister has stated frankly that no amount of influence and no prestigious appointment, is in any way a substitute for the satisfaction of holding supreme office. Yet such people are the exception. They are usually people of great ability whose scope has been frustrated. For, after all, what is it that retired Prime Ministers usually do when they retire? They settle down and write their memoirs. No doubt this is partly for their own pleasure. But it is also "to set the record straight", to give a particular version of the period in which the person held office. It is written with more than half an eye on historians who will write about the period. In other words, the retired ruler is not satisfied simply by the remembered pleasure of power. He, or she, wants to be well thought of by future generations, wants to be remembered as a Prime Minister who did great things, or at least who was not responsible for great disasters. This suggests that more fundamental than the pursuit of money or position or power is the desire to be well thought of.

We all have different interests and abilities but we are united in a desire to be recognized and valued. An old person leaves a party for the elderly complaining that the Vicar never spoke a word to her. She felt unrecognized and unappreciated. A dignitary at a formal dinner reflects to himself that he should be sitting at the top table with the more important people. He thinks of himself as someone who matters and is annoyed that other people do not seem to share his sense of his own importance. The feelings of such people are in no way different from those of a retired Prime Minister writing his or her memoirs for posterity or from the feelings of any of us. We like to be well thought of.

It is a drive that C. S. Lewis explored so brilliantly in his essay *The Inner Ring*. He showed how all our life we are conscious of a series of rings in our lives, by some of which we are included and others of which we are excluded. There is one group of friends that we feel very much part of, but "Mrs So-and-So? No, she really isn't one of us, she isn't on our wavelength." But then there is that group of people who always lunch together at the office. I'm never quite sure whether I'm wanted at their table. They always seem so smart and sophisticated. Perhaps that's a group that I'm excluded from? In my worse moments I talk about it being a clique. But it is a clique that I secretly regard as desirable. If I was in it I would regard it not as a clique but as a small group of rather nice, like-minded people.

In our time, aware as we are of the psychological dimension to everything, there is a tendency to account for this drive to be well thought of in terms of childhood deprivations. There is much truth in this explanation. Everyone knows that the people who are always trying to impress are in fact very insecure. They try to impress others because they are far from impressed with themselves. On the other hand, those who are of real ability have no need to draw everyone else's attention to it. If you are a good cricketer people can see you in action and read your batting average in the record books. If you are not, but would like to be, you have to use other methods to convince others, and yourself, such as recounting the times you made fifty in twenty minutes.

Even more fundamental than our need to be successful is our need to be loved. People who have been deprived of love in childhood compensate for this in adulthood in a variety of strange, disturbing and sometimes disruptive ways. One of the most brilliant films of all times is *Citizen Kane*, about a man who built up a huge fortune and a vast newspaper empire. He was not a happy man. The film ends with Kane saying, "Rosebud", and being reminded of a sledge he had owned as a child which had the name painted on it and which had brought him such fun. Kane's life was seen in retrospect as a vain attempt to recapture a lost childhood happiness.

Yet obvious as these points are, they hardly account for that fundamental drive to be well thought of which is shared by so many human beings. The form this takes reflects cultural variants. It leads the Japanese warrior class to commit hara-kiri rather than surrender. In the Middle Ages it was focussed in the concept of "honour", and this is still a powerful factor in Spanish-speaking countries, as reflected for example in Conrad's novel *Nostromo*. The form varies in that the kind of respect desired and the people from whom above all it is wanted, varies. The principle remains unchanged. To be human is to want "a good name". This applies as much in a terrorist group or the underworld of criminals as it does in an Inn of Court. What changes is the people by whom we want to be thought well of.

Our nature is fallen human nature, that is, we are born into and shaped by influences that are less than perfect. This means that our drives are always seeking distorted outlets. Yet the basic drive to be respected belongs to our being as such and is part of our God-given nature. It is part of that creation about which God said, "And behold it was good". Indeed, without it, we would not exist. For to exist is to exist with a drive to be someone, to make something of our life. Part of that drive takes the form of wanting to make something of our life in the eyes of someone else, wanting to be recognized and valued.

Affirmed but Wanting to Please

We seek success, and success is inseparable from the approval of those whose approval we covet. A Prime Minister looks to "the judgement of history", a serious painter or novelist hopes his works will survive and become part of the canon of English art or literature, a wife wants to remain in the fond memory of her husband, a father in the affection and respect of his children. Some Christian thought implies that we should discard this desire for success altogether. A well-known prayer of St Ignatius contains the lines: "Teach us to labour without seeking any reward save that of knowing that we do thy will." A noble sentiment and one to which we will return, but the teaching of Jesus is somewhat different from this. He said:

> When you give alms, sound no trumpet before you, as the hypocrites do in the synagogues and in the streets, that they may be praised by men. Truly, I say to you, they have their reward. But when you give alms, do not let your left hand know what your right hand is doing, so that your alms may be in secret; and your Father who sees in secret will reward you.[5]

Jesus repeated this teaching in relation to the other two traditional practices of religion, fasting and prayer. In each saying the point is the same. He does not say that we are to act without thought of reward. On the contrary, he assumes we do act with a view to something. The point is that if we act in order to win the praise of our fellow human beings, we have our reward already: "They have received their reward." We have got what we wanted, the attention and approval of people whom we judge to matter. Those who give money or fast or pray in secret, however, are known to God, and he will reward them.

This teaching does not preclude the possibility of doing action for its own intrinsic worth, or for the benefit of others. For we might say, "I am giving some money to that person simply because they need it", or "I am praying because I want to draw closer to God". The teaching does, however, challenge the idea that our actions can go unrewarded. The assumption is that our actions not only have an outcome but lead to the approval or disapproval of others. So the question is, whose approval do I desire, whose disapproval do I fear?

So far so simple. We all seek the respect and approval of someone. For most of the time we look to the judgement of our fellow human beings. Jesus teaches us to look to that of our heavenly father. At this point, however, the Christian faith brings in a complication. It tells us we already have the approval of our Heavenly Father. It is not something we have to strive for. The words which Jesus heard at his Baptism, "Thou art my beloved Son, with thee I am well pleased"[6] and which rang in his ears throughout his ministry, are, through him, to ring in our ears. Each one of us is a beloved son or daughter in whom God is well pleased. Not of course through any striving on our part but because we are "accepted in the beloved". This simple idea is absurdly difficult for people to grasp at an emotional level. Even people who have been religious all their lives, even converted Christians, sometimes find it difficult. It is one of the factors which prevents their happiness. They feel happiness must be earned, must come about only as a result of successful effort. But the emotion of happiness, if it comes at all, just comes: and if it comes it must just be accepted. This emotion of happiness is intimately bound up with being able to accept oneself, be oneself, and be glad about oneself simply because one is oneself.

The two approaches to this problem suggested here do not obviously fit together. One accepts that to seek the approval of someone is a fundamental part of our nature and urges us to seek the approval of God rather than man. The other says that we no longer need seek the approval of anyone, for God has set his seal of approval on us. All that is necessary is to accept God's acceptance of us and rejoice in being the person we are. Yet these two approaches are not mutually exclusive. In a family there are two daughters. One gives her mother a present in order to win an approval she fears she may not have. The other gives her mother a present out of the sense of approval she already feels. The first daughter is uncertain whether she is loved and gives to retain a love she fears she might lose. The other knows she is loved and gives as an expression of this love. The latter is a model of the Christian life. We do not have to win God's approval, for in Christ we are already approved of. Nevertheless, our action is still God-orientated. We look to him and give to him out of the love we feel and in response to it.

There is a strong "reward" element in the New Testament that cannot be ignored simply because it fits uncomfortably with our notion of doing something for its own sake without any thought of a reward at all. Jesus is more realistic than we are. He accepted that the desire for approval was part of our nature, as he accepted fear. Nevertheless, there is a distinction between intrinsic and extrinsic rewards. The latter, like medals pinned on the chest, have no essential connection with the action for which they are the reward. They may be valuable, but they are in the end arbitrary. Other forms of reward could have been chosen equally well. Intrinsic rewards, however, as the phrase suggests, have an integral connection with the action. When a couple save and plan for their future home, that home when they eventually find themselves married and in it, is what all their striving has led to. So God, and heaven, is the goal, the culmination, the fruition of the Christian life. It is not something tacked on the end for good conduct, but where the road has been leading and what the struggle has been about. For this reason the Christian orientates himself towards God, but not in order to earn or win anything. He wants to "please" God as love wants to please. When we give someone a present we want them to be pleased, to be happy. We are delighted if their face breaks into a genuine smile of pleasure. They are delighted and we are delighted. So in this way the loving soul seeks to please God.

Beyond the Ego-Trip

The striving for success is a stringy part of all of us. We want others to notice us and regard us as important. This striving cannot be eliminated simply by trying, as all those little stories about humility make clear. Three religious were arguing about the respective merits of their orders. The Dominican talked about the great intellectual tradition of the Dominicans, the Jesuit about the discipline of the Jesuits. Not to be outdone the Franciscan blurted out, "Ah, but when it comes to humility, we beat the lot of you." Another story concerns a schoolboy who was getting very cocky. The headmaster called him into his study and told him to go away and practise a little humility. Everything was fine for about a week and then the boy reverted to his old ways. "What went wrong?" said the head when he had the boy in his study again. "Well," said the boy, "I did practise humility for a week, but nobody noticed."

Humility cannot be acquired just by going for it. Indeed, just the opposite. Some of the most sophisticated and deep-set forms of pride hide under the guise of humility. Humility can cloak some hideous forms of arrogance. So the first and continuing task is to try to be as aware of our motivation as possible. We may despise all the goals other people seek, and have the most marvellous ideal of ourselves as someone who wants something totally different, but this in itself is not enough to change our nature. Malcolm Muggeridge, in a superb piece of sustained imagery, once wrote:

> Now the prospect of death overshadows all others. I am like a man on a sea voyage nearing his destination. When I embarked I worried about having a cabin with a porthole, whether I should be asked to sit at the captain's table, who were the more attractive and important passengers. All such considerations become pointless when I shall so soon be disembarking . . . the passion to accumulate possessions, or to be noticed and important, is too evidently absurd to be any longer entertained.[7]

Alas, the passion to accumulate possessions or to be noticed and important, though evidently absurd, does not for that reason or in response to that thought, necessarily become any less a part of our personality. Nor do old age or the prospect of death of themselves bring wisdom. So, we have to face that part of ourselves which still very much wants to have a cabin with a porthole, a seat at the captain's table, and which is all too aware of who are the more attractive and important passengers. Father H. A. Williams tells the story of a bishop who came to the vicarage door to offer the incumbent preferment (a clergy euphemism for promotion). The Vicar said he must go away and pray about it. The Vicar's wife went upstairs to pack. In characteristic fashion Father Williams suggests that the Vicar's wife was closer to God than her husband, for she was more honest about herself. We need not take this story as a moral not to pray about the jobs we are offered. We should so pray. We should also try to know the reality of our own human feelings.

Clergy are not always as aware as they might be of their

own hidden springs of action. Bernard Levin once did a dialogue in St Mary-le-Bow, which has two large pulpits specially built for this purpose. After he had finished a dialogue with the then Rector, Joseph McCulloch, he remarked that he was going straight out to buy a pulpit and install it in his own home for he had never felt such a sense of power in all his life. There is a power factor in all aspects of a clergyman's relationship with people, not only when he is preaching from the pulpit. It is a hazard of the trade. The struggle to dominate or avoid domination is a part of every relationship, not excluding that of a priest to his people. It is easy for priests (and devout Christians), who are dealing all the time in the coinage of absolute ideals like self-giving love, to confuse ideal and reality. The reality is that the human tendency to dominate and the ego with its attention-seeking devices is always present, and in religious people it takes a religious form. At a conference producers of religious programmes for television were asked what was the greatest hindrance to their work. "The vanity of the clergy" came the instant reply of the wisest man there.

The common view of the ordained ministry in the eighteenth and early nineteenth centuries was that it was a career like any other. Preferment had to be sought, as in any other department of life, through personal contacts and patronage. It was widely accepted that any healthy able young man would try to get to the top. It is this atmosphere that forms the background to *Barchester Towers*. A vacancy occurs in a bishopric and "A name began to be mentioned in high places". Due to the influence of the Evangelical and Oxford movements the Church is not now regarded as a profession in which a career may be advanced. This is all to the good and a return to more Dominical standards. Yet human ambitions and desires remain what they always were. If they cannot find one outlet they will look for another. Sometimes they take subtle forms and sometimes clergy are curiously blind. One young clergyman, arriving at a party and seeing another clergyman there, opened the conversation with the words, "Oh, I do hate clergymen, don't you?" Such a remark is curiously blind because it is obvious that clergymen hate clergymen; as doctors hate fellow doctors and teachers hate fellow teachers. It is a simple example of peer group rivalry exacerbated by the fact that a teacher knows all the tricks and vanities of being a teacher, as a doctor does of being a doctor and a clergyman of being a clergyman. No one knows the humbug, hypocrisy and vanity of being a clergyman better than the clergyman himself. Or he ought to. One sign that he doesn't is when he thinks he is different from other clergymen, somehow superior, as betrayed in the remark, "Oh, I do hate clergymen."

As there are particular hazards in being a priest so there are in being a layman. It is the same heart "deceitful above all things" finding a different form of deceit. One widespread form of egoism is the idea that we are somehow doing the Church or the clergyman or even God a favour by turning up for services. Chad Varah, the founder of the Samaritans, used to convey forcibly to the hundreds of people who turn up to be volunteers that they were not doing anyone a favour. On the contrary, if they were extremely lucky, a few of them might be selected as suitable for work with the Samaritans. For those few it would be a supreme privilege to be a volunteer, for in very few spheres of life is it possible to say that a person is doing some positive good. If this is so in relation to the Samaritans it is even more true in relation to the Church. It is a supreme privilege to be a member of Christ's Church and to receive the sacraments. This remains true however dispiriting the services may be, and often are; however banal the sermons may be, and often are; however petty and spiteful congregational life may be, and often is. To be given the gift of faith and grafted into the body of

Christ by baptism; to take one's place with other believers in the fellowship of the Spirit and to receive with them the food of angels, the bread of life, the very life of God himself – here is God's graciousness indeed. The problem of Christian egoism is not a new one. It forms the background of most of the letters in the New Testament. So Paul had to remind his readers of what remains true today:

> Not many of you were wise according to worldly standards, not many were powerful, not many were of noble birth; but God chose what is foolish in the world to shame the wise, God chose what is weak in the world to shame the strong, God chose what is low and despised in the world, even things that are not, to bring to nothing things that are, so that no human might boast in the presence of God.[8]

The only success is that which counts as success with God. Jesus made it quite clear that the attempt to put God first in our life is in continual conflict with other ambitions, in particular with our desire for money, power and fame. He also made it quite clear that there can be no compromise between God and these goals. His teaching is unequivocal:

> No one can serve two masters; for either he will hate the one and love the other, or he will be devoted to the one and despise the other. You cannot serve God and mammon.[9]

At another point he brought this teaching home to a particular person:

> And Jesus looking upon him loved him, and said to him, "You lack one thing; go, sell what you have, and give to the poor, and you will have treasure in heaven; and come, follow me."[10]

On the question of power and status Jesus was no less insistent: no compromise is possible between our desire to dominate and the selfless service of Christian discipleship.

> A dispute also arose among them, which of them was to be regarded as the greatest. And he said to them, "The kings of the Gentiles exercise lordship over them; and those in authority over them are called benefactors. But not so with you; rather let the greatest among you become as the youngest, and the leader as one who serves. For which is the greater, one who sits at table, or one who serves? Is it not the one who sits at table? But I am among you as one who serves."[11]

Our natural way of acting is to let others feel the weight of our authority (which is another translation of "exercise lordship") but "It shall not be so with you."

The teaching of Jesus is related to the actual forces which drive us, money, power and fame, the last named already having been referred to in the teaching on prayer, fasting and almsgiving. The message is uncompromising.

> If your right eye causes you to sin, pluck it out and throw it away; it is better that you lose one of your members than that your whole body be thrown into hell. And if your right hand causes you to sin, cut it off and throw it away; it is better that you lose one of your members than that your whole body go into hell.[12]

The problem is that however much we assent in theory to the absolute priority to be accorded God over every other human ambition, we remain desperately divided in our loyalties. Malcolm Muggeridge brings this out well in his description of Beatrice Webb, based upon what she herself revealed of herself in her diaries:

In partnership with Sidney, she was a public figure concerned with public affairs; writing her diary, she was alone with her thoughts, her longings, and sometimes her God. If she had married Joseph Chamberlain, the love of her life, she would have been a great hostess; if she had given herself wholly to teaming up with Sidney, she would have been a great behind-the-scenes political operator; if she opted for God, she would have been a twentieth century St Teresa of Avila.

As it was, she dithered between all three; letting her mind dwell on Chamberlain when she had abolished him from her life; treading in Sidney's tiny footsteps, or, better, manfully pedalling behind him on their bicycle-made-for-two; slipping into Westminster Abbey to pray long and earnestly to a God she no longer believed in.[13]

The state of most of us is rather worse than that of Beatrice Webb – and we are less aware of it. Yet in our better moments we know this won't do. If we are to achieve anything, even in human terms, single-mindedness is necessary. During the North Africa campaign in the 1939–45 war, an inscription was found which read:

I, the captain of a Legion of Rome, serving in the Desert of Libya, have learnt and pondered this truth: there are in life but two pursuits, love and power, and no one has both.[14]

In affairs of the heart it is notorious that it is not possible to pursue two relationships simultaneously. Yet time and again human beings fail to be resolute enough to give up one in order to make a success of the other. The result is that they fail in both. The realists are those who, if they find themselves caught in two mutually exclusive relationships, are single-minded enough to break off one.

In affairs of the heart a resoluteness bordering on ruthlessness (with oneself) is necessary in order that at least one ship might sail. What is true in human relationship is even more so in our relationship with God. Those who have served God best have often taken a step, at one stage in their lives, which seems horrifying to us. There is a distinguished churchman who was once a professional artist. On becoming a Christian in adult life he burnt all his paintings. Gerard Manley Hopkins in 1868 burnt all he had ever written, resolving "to write no more, as not belonging to my profession, unless it were by the wish of my superiors." For seven years he wrote nothing. Such single-minded resolution and ruthless putting aside of what appears at the time to conflict with the priority of God in our life, applies in different ways at different stages in our life. In every life there are certain decisive turning points. One usually occurs in middle age. There is certainly another in old age. The successive review and re-ordering of our life which is necessary need not be dramatic in the world's terms but it can be painful. A member of a congregation, in his sixties, reviewing his expenditure and life-style, decided to resign from all his golf clubs, tennis clubs and so on. He wanted to re-orientate his life and this was one small aspect of the turning.

Richness Within

When a person whose goals in life have been money, power and fame comes up against the teaching of Christ he can only be aware of an absolute gulf between what he has previously considered desirable and the total claim of God, where our surpassing happiness lies. So it is not surprising that according to the teaching of Jesus the rule of God in human affairs will bring about a complete reversal. The first will be last and the last will be first. The poor, those who have nothing and know they have nothing, are those to whom the kingdom belongs; the meek inherit the earth. Nevertheless, it is a misreading of the Bible to think that success, in a Christian sense, is confined to heaven. First, the New Testament should not be read in isolation from the Old. In the Old Testament God's blessing is shown on this earth in very tangible ways.

> Thou visitest the earth, and blessest it: thou makest it very plenteous.
>
> Thou crownest the year with thy goodness: and thy clouds drop fatness.
>
> They shall drop upon the dwellings of the wilderness: and the little hills shall rejoice on every side.
>
> The folds shall be full of sheep: the valleys also shall stand so thick with corn, that they shall laugh and sing.[15]
>
> Lord, lift thou up the light of thy countenance upon us. Thou hast put gladness in my heart since the time that their corn, and wine, and oil, increased.[16]

When things go well with us this is a sign of God's blessing. It does not follow that if things go badly this is a sign of God's disapproval. That false step was sometimes taken in both Judaism and Calvinism. But Calvinism, for all the way it has been twisted and despite the bad image it has come to have because of the association of its ideas with the rise of capitalism, points to an Old Testament insight that the Church has sometimes lost sight of. God's blessing includes well-being and success in material affairs. The New

Testament also indicates this, for all the radical nature of the demands it puts before us. In his teaching on anxiety Christ told his followers not to worry about what they would have to eat or what they would wear, "Your heavenly Father knows that you need them all. But seek first his kingdom and his righteousness, and all these things shall be yours as well."[17] There is no doubt that we are to seek God's will and strive to have it realized on earth before anything else. Nevertheless "all these things", those things which are necessary for us, will be added unto us as well. When Peter told Christ that the disciples had left everything to follow him, Christ told him that not only would he be blessed in the new world but:

Everyone who has left houses or brothers or sisters or father or mother or children or lands, for my name's sake, will receive a hundredfold, and inherit eternal life. But many that are first will be last, and the last first.[18]

This imagery is not to be taken literally any more than the reference to plucking out the eye or cutting off the hand. Nevertheless the import is clear: God's blessing is to be expected in material as well as spiritual ways.

When should this blessing be expected? That we do not know and cannot know. For faith is trust and any attempt to tie God down to particular times and occasions would be magic or worse: worse because it would involve control and manipulation of God who is sovereign in his freedom. God's blessing in tangible, material ways might be shown soon. Or it might take a long time. The poetry of Gerard Manley Hopkins was not known in his lifetime. It was published after his death by his friend Robert Bridges and only became widely known in this century. Thomas Traherne, though he was known in his own time for some of his theological writings, did not have his poetry and meditations, which we appreciate, discovered for nearly three hundred years. Julian of Norwich had to wait eight hundred years to be properly recognized as one of the great mystics of all time. From the fourteenth century until the twentieth she was virtually unknown. The blessing which God bestows on those who give up all to follow him is certainly made known on this earth. His word does not return void: but we do not know the times and the seasons.

Success is success according to God. Here the Christian is conscious of a paradox. For in one profound sense he is no longer concerned with success at all. For success is about winning the respect and esteem of those whose judgement we most value: and we are already pronounced blessed; we are already accepted in the beloved. The first priority for a Christian is simply to become more deeply conscious of the reality of God and his love for us. As Monica Furlong has put it:

> The most difficult and worthwhile feat of all is to become so rich inside ourselves that we become careless of other forms of wealth and status. The richness and stillness out of which it comes, really makes it possible to love others.[19]

It is by becoming rich inside ourselves that we come to sit light to what the world regards as important. This inner transformation, though it can only come about by divine grace, involves us in a costly discipleship. For the Christian faith is not about a cosy and vague feeling. It is about a God made known to us in the absolute claims and promises of Christ. Again, these claims are not vague and general but related to the specific goals that human beings seek, money, power and fame. For this reason the disciple of Christ will experience a number of crisis points in this life where a choice has to be made. In the process our whole understanding of success becomes changed. A Welsh minister once explained how during the first part of his training success was seen purely in terms of passing exams. Then he went on to another college and the Professor asked him to write an essay on the divinity of Christ. He spent six weeks over it and was quite pleased with the result when he took it in for the Professor to read. As he read the essay the Professor sighed from time to time. Then he asked the intending minister, "I think I know as much about Barth and Brunner as you?" to which the reply could only be Yes. The Professor then knelt down, with the essay in hand, and exclaimed, "The Reverend T. J. Davis, BA, henceforth I commend you to the flames." He then threw the essay in the fire with the words "ashes to ashes, dust to dust". The intending minister was astonished and not a little chagrined. He was then the recipient of a personal sermon on the importance of mixing his words with a touch of the soil, with the object of trying to convey the reality of Christ rather than display academic prowess.

In one way or another we are all faced with the challenge to seek first the Kingdom of God and to surrender our cherished human goals: to work for what is right in God's eye and to sit light to what passes for human success.

✠

God of all goodness, grant us to desire ardently,
to seek wisely, to know surely,
and to accomplish perfectly
thy holy will,
for the glory of thy name.

(St Thomas Aquinas)

O God, complete in yourself,
you have yet surrendered your self-sufficiency to
    make us, creatures of your love:
made us able to thwart your purposes,

able to hurt you.
O God, most perfect love become most vulnerable,
help us to share in and not spoil
your great work.

NOTES

1. T. S. Eliot, *The Complete Poems and Plays*, Faber 1969, p. 258.
2. Remark made to Deirdre Bair, Deidre Bair *Samuel Beckett*, Cape 1978, p. 640.
3. Boswell's *Life of Johnson*, Everyman, Vol. II, p. 132
4. ibid, Vol. I, p. 532.
5. Matthew 6:2–4.
6. Mark 1:9.
7. Malcolm Muggeridge, "Credo" in *Jesus Rediscovered*, Fount 1969, pp. 57f.
8. 1 Corinthians 1:26–9.
9. Matthew 6:24.
10. Mark 10:21.
11. Luke 22:24–7
12. Matthew 5:29–30.
13. *The Times*, 9 October 1982.
14. Quoted by Malcolm Muggeridge in above article.
15. Psalm 65:9–13.
16. Psalm 4:6–7.
17. Matthew 6:32–3.
18. Matthew 19:29–30.
19. Monica Furlong, *Contemplating Now*, Hodder & Stoughton 1971, p. 128.

FOR DISCUSSION

1. What do the very varied attempts of human beings to achieve success have in common?

2. Is it possible to be both a faithful Christian and highly successful in this world's terms?

3. How do we become "rich inside ourselves" and so "careless of other forms of wealth and status"?

6.

Security

The Precariousness of Human Life

At certain times of the year we seem especially aware of accidents. In July or August, when many people are travelling on holiday, and when there is often a shortage of other news, we read about coach crashes on crowded motorways, plane crashes with many killed, helicopters sinking in the sea with a number drowned; about swimmers drowned in rivers and the sea; about boats lost at sea; about people killed in storms, floods and by lightning. Accidents are in the air and life seems highly precarious. Yet this is, of course, the permanent condition of mankind. Every day people are killed on the roads. Every day people drop dead in the street with heart attacks. Every day houses go up in flames, and the occupants with them. Furthermore, it could be argued that despite all this people in England, for example, are a great deal more secure than those living in other parts of the world where there is the constant threat of war, revolution, terrorism, plague and murder. The precariousness of human life is one of its most fundamental features.

There are two possible attitudes to this frightening insecurity. We can pretend it does not exist or we can face it. There are many ways of pretending that it does not exist. We can simply block out all news of illness and accident, for example. This is difficult to do, and so the most common device is to live on the assumption that such misfortune strikes other people down, not oneself. Of course we know in theory that if accidents occur they can involve me. Yet in fact we tend to live on the assumption that it is always someone else to whom these things happen.

In our better moments we don't want to be ostrich-like, with our head in the sand. We want to be mature. We want to face the worst that life has to offer and somehow learn to live with the thought and cope with the possibility. At this point quite a number of people do in fact act with sense and prudence. They make a will and, if they can afford it, take out an insurance policy or otherwise make some provision for any dependants there might be. Even so it is surprising how many people die intestate. They have not been able to face the thought of their own demise even to the extent of making a will.

The next step is more difficult. It means accepting that what we have long dreamt of and planned for may not come about. There are many people who look forward to their retirement. They work hard and they long for the time when they will have more leisure and be able to do all those things they would like to do. Yet every week we hear of someone who has died within a year of retiring. Perhaps they overworked and when they retired the toll for so many years of strain on the system was exacted. We need to build an element of detachment into our outlook, an inner "If I am spared that long". One headmaster always prefaces all school timetables with the initials DV – *Deo Volente*, if God is willing. It is a healthy reminder that life contains the unexpected and unpredictable and so our best laid plans can go astray.

Facing the insecurity of life has at its heart facing the prospect of our own death. We joke about this and this joking has a healthy element to it, for humour is a form of acceptance and a way of accepting things. Nevertheless there is an inescapable element of fear present. Not many modern people admit to a fear of death itself, but most admit to a fear of the process of dying. However much good news we hear about the work of hospices enabling our end to be painless and peaceful, the thought of the process of our own dying is not a pleasant one. No wonder we joke about it. So Woody Allen, "I'm not frightened of dying, I just don't want to be there when it happens, that's all." John Mortimer wrote about the death of his remarkable blind father in the following words:

> The huge and unwieldy garden surrounding the small house seemed unnaturally silent and I could hear nothing but the sound of my father's assisted breathing. At the last moment he wanted to get out of bed and cried out angrily because we wouldn't let him have a bath. When my mother protested he said, "I'm always angry when I'm dying". I don't know if it was something he had prepared for a long time, but those were the last words I heard him say. I held the mask over his face until he no longer had need of it.[1]

"I'm always angry when I'm dying" is a lovely example of the way we both face and don't face our fear; the way we both accept and don't accept our own death. Terror and anger are transmuted into a humour that accepts them; but not totally.

Facing up to our own death has been the advice of poets, novelists, moralists, religious guides, would-be philosophers and friends in every age. In religious terms it has taken the form of injunctions to live each day as if it were our last and to practise dying. All this is sound enough, though not easy. Together with this has gone the message that it is in God himself, and in him alone, that our true security lies. This is true, though before exploring further what this means it is necessary to raise one or two niggling doubts.

Why Such Insecurity?

First, why has God placed us in a world of such radical insecurity? It is not an adequate answer to point out that much of the insecurity is of our own making. Leaving aside illness, very many of the accidents that befall us are in principle avoidable, if not by ourselves at least by those responsible. Nevertheless God did not need to have total knowledge of the future to know that the possibility of accident is inherent in the very business of living. Parents when they bring children into the world are highly aware of this, so we cannot say less of God. We have in fact to say that God knowingly placed us in an environment where there is always the possibility of sudden death. Why? We need as it were a theology of insecurity. The only possible answer that is compatible with belief in a loving God is that (a) he has something more than finite security in mind for us, and (b) in order that we might be receptive to the possibility of receiving this ultimate security, it is necessary that we do not find everything we want in the created order. Security on this earth would mean not simply that we are protected from a particular illness or accident but that we never die. Even if our death was ten thousand years away, time would pass and one day we would feel its shadow. And if we were designed to live for ever on this earth what would there be to lift our minds to something better? We would be relatively content with what we had. God has designed us not simply for life but for eternal life, a life which is both quantitatively and qualitatively different from finite existence. No other explanation is compatible with a faith in a good God.

Two further niggles arise out of this answer. First, any prospect of eternity tends to suggest to the modern mind that this will lead to people being less interested in or committed to the world we know. Marx, Freud and others have sowed serpent's teeth in the modern mind. But there is no necessary connection between belief in eternity and sitting light to the responsibilities and duties of this life. On the contrary, many would argue, and many more show by their lives, that it is the light of eternity that enables us to see this life in its proper perspective. The light of eternity shines on the things and people of this world in such a way as both to bring out and enhance their natural value. Secondly, there is a sneaking feeling that the offer of an eternal life is too good to be true, or as Iris Murdoch put it, "Anything that consoles is fake." But the statement that anything that consoles is fake, is not an argument, it is an unproven assumption. The contrary assertion "anything that does not console is fake" is equally true and equally unproven. If the assertion "anything that consoles is fake" expresses a fear of the power of wishful thinking to distort reality, it can also betray a perverse desire to have an unhappy rather than a happy ending.

God knowingly created us as vulnerable flesh and blood creatures and placed us in a world of radical insecurity. In this way he keeps our minds and hearts open for the ultimate security to be found in relation to himself. But is not insecurity a bad thing? We want our children to feel secure. We want them not only to know that they are loved but to feel that they live in a safe environment. We think it odd if parents spend all their time telling their young children about the horrors of life. We recognize that though children have to be made aware of the dangers of human life it would be wrong and psychologically unhealthy for them to be brought up with the idea that life consists of people, including children, dying all the time. Parents are right to want to protect their children; nevertheless, as we grow older we do become more and more aware of the precariousness of human life. And though this is disturbing and unsettling, there is in fact just enough security to enable us both to plan and to live. Life is a growth into greater awareness and this is the way God meant it to be. We begin in the womb, very secure and almost totally unaware. We are born, many of us, into a protected environment and are to a great extent protected as children. As we grow older we become more conscious of the character of existence in all its beauty and horror. Often we wish life was of a rather different character, yet even an eighty-year-old plans the day on the assumption that he or she is going to live to the end of it. The person may be highly aware of living on the edge and be ready for death yet still able to live a properly human life. Marianne Thornton wrote of William Wilberforce in old age:

> I wish you could have seen him as he stood under the Tulip trees telling of . . . many of whom he has seen pass and re-pass amongst our shades – "And they are gone – and here am I" he said, "a wreck left for the next tide – but yet abounding in blessings and enjoyments."[2]

Our ultimate security is in God himself. The thought is superbly expressed in Psalm 91, the psalm sung in the late evening service of Compline:

> Thou shalt not be afraid for any terror by night
>> nor for the arrow that flieth by day;
> For the pestilence that walketh in darkness:
>> nor for the sickness that destroyeth in the noon-day.
> A thousand shall fall beside thee,
>> and ten thousand at thy right hand:
> but it shall not come nigh thee.

What the psalmist affirmed so confidently cannot be literally true. We do get struck down by arrows, or their modern equivalent, disease and accident. Nor can we assume that God is so selective that he would save us and allow our ten thousand neighbours to perish. But what the psalm says is true in an even more important sense. "For thou, Lord, art my hope" it goes on to say. God is our hope in two ways. First, though everything changes one thing does not change: God and his undeviating good-will towards us. Through Christ and in Christ we are taken into a relationship to God that from his side never falters. Secondly, we have a future in him. This future may be unimaginable but we have it on his promise, it is affirmed in Christ, and the nature of love suggests, that our relationship to God does not end at death. Who we are is a mystery. But we can rest assured that whoever we are we are fully known to God; and whatever happens to our physical frame, his knowledge of us does not end at death. He will recreate or reform us in the stuff of glory, in a form appropriate to an eternal form of existence.

If God is our hope, if we have an unimaginably marvellous future in him, it might be logical to look forward to death. Nevertheless, we are all different, and psychological factors play an important part here. Some people have indeed longed for death. Stevie Smith is a good modern example:

> Ah me, sweet Death, you are the only god
> Who comes as a servant when he is called, you know,
> Listen then to this sound I make, it is sharp,
> Come Death, do not be slow.[3]

This was written when Stevie Smith had had a stroke and it was the last poem she wrote. As such it is understandable enough, though all her life she had a longing to die. This longing to die was not an expression of her religious faith, which was ambivalent, but was obviously related to psychological factors. In contrast Catherine Bramwell-Booth, the devout grand-daughter of the founder of the Salvation Army, said this on the occasion of her hundredth birthday:

It's a very strange experience, living so near to death as I do now. I know it must be next door, tomorrow perhaps, or even today. But I don't want to die. Ought I to feel guilty about that? I don't want to die as I'm in love with life.[4]

Whether we want to die depends upon personal factors outside our control. What matters is that we should be ready to die and that in the event of dying we should be able to commit ourselves trustingly into the hands of God.

Facing Death Before it Comes

In the past there has been much stress on not dying suddenly or unprepared. The Litany of the 1662 Anglican Prayer Book has the refrain:

From battle and murder, and from sudden death, *Good Lord, deliver us.*

In Graham Greene's novel *Brighton Rock* one of the characters has the adage "Between the wheel and the road" running through his mind. It is a reminder to himself that even in the time it takes to go under the wheel of a car, in that split second, there is time to make peace with God. This is clearly a theme with great dramatic possibilities (which, for example, Evelyn Waugh exploited in *Brideshead Revisited*); and there is Gospel truth in it. The story of the penitent thief in the passion story is a standing reminder that it is never too late to turn to Christ. Nevertheless, the Christian is not primarily concerned whether his death is sudden or lingering. However it comes he will want to be in a state of readiness.

Earlier ages kept us in a state of readiness through various *memento mori*. These often took the form of a skull and crossbones on a gravestone and some suitable epithet to the fact that you, cheerful walker-by, had better look at this for soon you will be just as much dust and ashes as the dead person here commemorated. For example, in All Saints', Fulham's old parish church, there is a memorial to Sir William Butts, Henry VIII's doctor, who is mentioned by Shakespeare. There is the usual skull and crossbones, and the inscription when translated reads:

> Of what worth is medicine, honour, royal favour, the love of the people, where cruel death comes? Piety, which is built on Christ the Founder alone helps us. It alone in death avails: all other things pass away. Therefore, when Christ has to me been everything in life, death, for me will be a gain, and Christ will be life.[5]

Other devices were primarily concerned to remind the deceased, when still alive, that they had to die. Some people, for example, when they had their reclining figure carved in stone had another figure of themselves carved at the same time but this one as a skeleton. Both these figures would be carved in a person's lifetime and one would go below the other. There is a good example of this in the church of Brou in the south of Burgundy in France. The monument in the church shows magnificently clothed figures of Philibert and Marguerite of Bourbon reclining on the top deck of a stone bunk. In the bunks beneath are their carved skeletons.

Such monuments are interesting and amusing, though they are not as a rule to our taste as a way of making ourselves face up to mortality. Yet we know we must and the wisest of us do. In the summer of 1983 David Nye, his wife and three daughters, were killed in the Scillies helicopter crash. Shortly before this he had written a signed editorial for the

Bank of England staff magazine containing the words:

> The death of a relation, one dearly loved, focuses the thoughts on the inescapable movement forward to life. Such a sorrow forces home the realization that our existence allows no escape from change, from the unexpected, from the whole range of life's possibilities, from comedy to deepest tragedy. Experience dispels what one might call the Blandings Castle illusion, that perpetual Shropshire summer is humanly attainable. For even as the mallet swings and the croquet ball glides through the hoop into a patch of evening sunlight, in the midst of such domestic peace, time opens the crevasse at our feet. We none of us know, however secure behind the love of those around us, or bolstered by power and possessions, what even the next moment may mean to us. To imagine otherwise is to be, at the very least, unprepared.

How can we make these moving words a practical reality? The most effective and realistic method is through an acceptance of the losses we experience; loss of youth, loss of health, loss of mobility, loss of independence. The whole being revolts against this loss and from one point of view is right to do so. It is the reaction of a healthy, life-loving person against what diminishes and destroys us. This attitude was well expressed by some words of Dylan Thomas on the death of his father, which have since become well-known:

> Do not go gentle into that good night,
> Old age should burn and rave at close of day;
> Rage, rage, against the dying of the light.[6]

These words were quoted by Simone de Beauvoir on the first page of the book she wrote about her mother, *Une Mort Très Douce* (*A Happy Death* in the English version). The title is a bitter one. The mother, a practising Catholic, died of cancer. The theme of the book is stated in the final words:

> There is no such thing as a natural death: nothing that happens to man is ever natural because his very presence calls the world in question. Every man is mortal; but for every man his death is an accident and even if he knows of it and consents to it, an untimely violence.

This attitude is understandable. Indeed there is something biblical about it, for there is a strand of thinking in the Bible which regards death as "an enemy". Furthermore, in the last few decades theologians have often contrasted the way Socrates met his death – calmly, looking forward to the release of the soul from the body – with the attitude of Jesus. In the Garden of Gethsemane Jesus was "very sorrowful, even to death" and according to Luke his sweat was like great drops of blood falling to the ground. Three times he prayed that the cup of suffering and death might be removed from him. "Abba, Father, all things are possible to thee; remove this cup from me."

This attitude is understandable, healthy and biblical. But it is not the fullness of the biblical view. Jesus himself, according to Luke's account, died with the words "Father, into thy hands I commit my spirit" on his lips, words expressive of trust, acceptance, serenity. Furthermore we must ask, if death is simply an outrage, an "untimely violence", why did God create the world knowing that every creature would have to submit to its claim? God created the world. He created the world knowing we would have to die. Moreover, he created the world knowing that the creatures he would bring into existence would be aware that they would have to die. It is only consistent to say that God deliberately made us as creatures who would have to face inevitable death and that he did this in order to serve a particular purpose. Death is absolutely certain. This meant that God designed existence with both life and death clearly in mind. The only faith which will carry conviction is one in which life and death are integrated in one overall perspective. Support for the idea that this is possible comes from a surprising source, namely D. H. Lawrence. As he lay dying of TB in 1929, still only in his early forties, Lawrence wrote some of the most positive poems on death this century.

> Sing the song of death, O sing it!
> for without the song of death, the song of life
> becomes pointless and silly.[7]

If the refrain "Sing the song of death" had come from Stevie Smith we would be suspicious for she was in love with death as a way out of the misery of life. But Lawrence loved life, no less so than when he was singing the song of death. After his death his wife Frieda wrote, "Right up to the last he was *alive* and we both made the best of our days, then he faced the end so splendidly, and so like a *man*."[8]

Lawrence believed it was possible to sing the song of death because its shadow enables new growth to take place. In his remarkable poem *Shadows* he wrote:

> I am in the hands of the unknown God,
> he is breaking me down to his own oblivion
> to send me forth on a new morning, a new man.[9]

Lawrence was a religious man though not a Christian believer. What he was feeling after is made explicit within the Christian faith. Austin Farrer made the point in a sermon preached in the 1950s when a mission was going on in the University of Oxford, and he asked his congregation to consider the question of their unbelieving friends. Those nice but worldly friends: are they languishing for ever in hell? It seems absurd when we are all laughing together over a pint of beer in a pub. But, as Farrer said, man's destiny consists not of one but two parts:

> First we live then we die . . . In the eyes of God our dying is not simply negative, it is an immensely important and salutary thing; by living we become ourselves, by dying we become God's, if, that is, we know how to die; if we so die, then everything we have become in our living is handed back to God who gave us life, for him to refashion and use according to his pleasure.
>
> God desires that we should grow, live, expand, enrich our minds and our imaginations, become splendid creatures. He also desires that we should die, should be crucified on the cross of Christ Jesus, should surrender all we have and are to him; and he desires that we should die that death spiritually before we die it physically.
>
> Well, now, what after all are we to say about our dear, delightful, unconverted friends? We must say that so far as their lives are wholesome or truly human, they are splendid manifestations of the power to live; but that they have not yet learned to die, they have not made even the first step along that more difficult path which Jesus Christ opened up for us.[10]

Yet, we still want to ask why should we "surrender all we have and are to him"? First, because God is the highest we know, the source and standard of all that we hold to be good, true and beautiful. Haunted and drawn by this absolute perfection we acknowledge it and offer to it the best we have. Secondly, because moment by moment we depend for our very being on this reality. We spring from his creative hand and without that hand there would be nothing. Our dependence on a source of being beyond ourselves is a fundamental constituent of reality. Dependence, not as immaturity but as admission of reality, is the only attitude which enables us to relate correctly to the universe. We receive our life as gift, sheer gift; and whatever there is beyond death is, likewise, sheer gift. Thirdly, because the threat of death comes to us blazoned with the promise "not less but more". God takes away only to bless more abundantly.

These three points taken together mean that the forces of decay and diminishment which culminate in death are not to be seen as negative and destructive. Though from one point of view what we experience is loss, from the other side this is a clearing of the ground in order that a greater gift still might be bestowed. Yeats expressed the challenge well in one of his poems:

> An aged man is but a paltry thing,
> a tattered coat upon a stick, unless
> soul clap its hands and sing, and louder sing
> For every tatter in its mortal dress.[11]

"Every tatter in its mortal dress" is that process of physical decline that begins in our mid-twenties and whose slope becomes so steep in later life. It is not only illness and mental slowing up that we have to face; it is physical constriction, gradually getting boxed in. At the end of John's Gospel Peter is told:

> When you were young, you girded yourself and walked where you would; but when you are old, you will stretch out your hands, and another will gird you and carry you where you do not wish to go.[12]

This passage refers to Peter's death by crucifixion. It also has a wider reference because for all of us life is a process in which we are more and more at the mercy of forces outside ourselves, forces which box us in. The most obvious example is that of a person who first finds he cannot walk as far as he once did, who becomes housebound, then bedridden and finally experiences a stroke which leaves him immobile, helpless and speechless. This final scene is presaged in every ache, twinge and feeling of tiredness. Yet, however difficult, this whole process can be transformed from an invasion by the forces of destruction to the welcomed entry of the liberating God. In so far as this is able to happen death has already been defeated even before it comes onto the field for the final battle. This is what St Paul referred to when he said "though our outer nature is wasting away, our inner nature is being renewed every day. For this slight momentary affliction is preparing for us an eternal weight of glory beyond all comparison" (2 Corinthians 4:16–17). A few verses earlier, talking about how the apostles were afflicted but not crushed, he said that they were "always carrying in the body the death of Jesus, so that the life of Jesus may also be manifested in our bodies."

This idea of death being defeated at every moment of our lives, through the whole process of dissolution that begins almost as soon as we are adult, was memorably put by Shakespeare in one of his sonnets:

Poor soul, the centre of my sinful earth,
My sinful earth these rebel pow'rs that thee array,
Why dost thou pine within and suffer dearth,
Painting thy outward walls so costly gay?
Why so large cost, having so short a lease,
Dost thou upon thy fading mansions spend?
Shall worms, inheritors of this excess,
Eat up thy charge? Is this thy body's end?
Then, soul, live thou upon thy servant's loss,
And let that pine to aggravate thy store;
Buy terms divine in selling hours of dross;

Within be fed, without be rich no more.
So shall thou feed on Death, that feeds on men,
And, Death once dead, there's no more dying then.[13]

"Death once dead, there's no more dying then"

A moving example of how we can "feed on Death, that feeds on men"; of how we can so live that death is defeated before it comes, was seen in John Robinson, the former Bishop of Woolwich, who died in December 1983. About two years before he died he preached at the funeral of a sixteen-year-old girl who had died of cancer. He told a somewhat shocked congregation that God is to be found in cancer as much as in a sunset. When he himself was diagnosed as having the same disease he discovered for himself the truth of what he had preached. He suggested three ways in which he had discovered God in his cancer. First, it set him thinking about the cause of cancer. He did not know the cause but he did know that hidden resentments and unresolved conflicts within us sometimes make their presence felt through physical illness. His cancer made him look at what he called his "unfinished agenda" and to face, come to terms with – and stronger that that – embrace things about himself he had tended to hide away. This reflection is the work of the Spirit of God who searches us out and knows us, leading us into the truth about ourselves and into a true love for ourselves.

Secondly, he became aware of the many people who cared for him. No doubt, he said, it was all there before but as a result of the cancer he had become aware, through the giving and receiving in relationships with his family and friends, of grace upon grace. Thirdly, when he was given only a few months to live he re-examined his priorities and decided to do only what really mattered. He went on holiday with his wife, he finished off some scholarly work and above all he tried to make his life really life, life with a capital L and not mere existence. This life, which the New Testament calls Eternal Life, is "begun, continued but not ended now". It is not ended with death, yet it has to begin in the here and now.

In these three ways John Robinson said he had found God in his cancer as much as in the sunset. We get lost if we try to work out why horrible things happen to some people and not to others. The golfer Ballesteros, a deeply religious man, was due to travel in the plane which crashed in Spain in December 1983, a crash in which all lives were lost. At the last moment he switched tickets. He blessed God but we wonder about the person who got his ticket at the last moment. There is no answer to the intellectual questions that arise in relation to such situations. What we do have is a practical answer in the living and dying of someone like John Robinson. In every situation, including our own dissolution, we can find God and co-operate with him in bringing forth some unique good from our pain and muddle and tragedy. St Paul wrote, "We know that in everything God works for good with those who love him."[14] This is quite different from saying that everything happens for the best. Manifestly everything that happens is not for the best. Yet in everything God is at work bringing out something better than what was once judged the best. We are finite, God is infinite. Our understanding of "the best" is always a horizon, at once a limitation on what we can see and a sign of something beyond, that we cannot yet see. As we approach God the horizon opens up before us endlessly, transfiguring all that we have previously known and understood to be "the best".

The current view of life is that it is a process of physical growth followed by physical decline. We work with Shakespeare's seven ages of man, from mewling infancy through to shrunk shank and slippered pantaloon, via bearded bravery in the cannon's face. In contrast to this the

Christian faith sets before us the prospect of physical and spiritual growth followed by further spiritual growth in proportion to our physical decline. Few people seem able to get the balance right. Either they affirm all that is healthy and life-giving and treat the later stages of life as sheer tragedy. Or they know God can be found in suffering and this leads them to underplay the way in which he is found in what is strong and healthy; and that his desire to bless us with somethng more than physical well-being is in no way a belittling, but rather a building on to what he first gives us. One of the few people who have achieved the right balance, in addition to Austin Farrer in the passage already quoted, was Teilhard de Chardin. In his spiritual classic *Le Milieu Divin* he described and affirmed how God can be known in all the activities of life, in all that makes for growth, development, maturity and well-being. But he believed with no less conviction that God can be known in what he called the forces of diminishment, in our passivities.

If God can shine out in people as a result of the forces of diminishment, we might expect that the older a person becomes the more transparent to God they will be. This is quite clearly not the case. There is no automatic link between ageing and growth in godliness. Rather, ageing tends to reveal us ever more starkly in our essential character, in our bitterness as well as our humility. T. S. Eliot wrote:

> Do not let me hear
> Of the wisdom of old men, but rather of their folly,
> Their fear of fear and frenzy, their fear of possession
> Of belonging to another; or to others, or to God.
> The only wisdom we can hope to acquire
> Is the wisdom of humility: humility is endless.[15]

Qualities which we view with a certain amused tolerance in youth, such as vanity or egoism, become grotesque in old age. There are few things in life so distasteful as the vanity of old people or the still prickly egoism of the aged. On the other hand, there are few things in life so moving as the characters of those who have used the process of growing old to grow into God. H. A. Williams brings this out in his description of the portrait of an old woman:

The same glimpse of resurrection can be seen in the portrait of an old woman by a contemporary painter of genius. The old woman's face is deeply lined as though it had been ploughed up again and again by agony upon agony. It is the face of somebody whom life has tortured without mercy. The furrows speak of wounds and deeper wounds, of sufferings and cares piled one on top of the other. It is the face of somebody who has found life an experience of continuous betrayal. The old woman looks as if no sorrow has passed her by, as though she could never be surprised again by any kind or degree of pain. Yet in his portrayal of this agonizingly tragic face, the artist has given an over-all impression of triumph. In its very lines and furrows the face gives off an invincible strength. The old woman possesses a wisdom and serenity which nothing can take from her. She is in possession of true and indestructible riches. She has looked on the travail of her soul and is satisfied. She is at peace – the peace which can belong only to those who are fully and deeply alive. What the artist has shown is victory over suffering by its acceptance – not the passive acceptance of hopeless resignation, but the active acceptance of one who has been willing to receive her suffering and absorb it and thus to make it contribute powerfully to what she is. The portrait shows somebody who has become fully a person by means of those very hammer-blows of experience which might have broken her up completely. Yet the face shows little conscious knowledge of her achievement. Her triumph is too real for her to be aware of it much. She is far beyond the stage of seeking artificial boosts in any narcissistic self-congratulation.[16]

That this is not simply an artist's imagination is shown in the description by Malcolm Muggeridge of someone he met at Lourdes even before he had become a believer. He went in a highly sceptical frame of mind but wrote in these terms about someone he met there who was dying:

> Like any other glib child of twentieth-century enlightenment I had nothing to say, until I noticed in the most extraordinarily vivid way, as in some girl with whom I had suddenly fallen in love, that her eyes were quite fabulously luminous and beautiful. What marvellous eyes! As I said this, the three of us – the dying woman, her sister and I – were somehow caught up in a kind of ecstasy . . . It was as though I saw God's love shining down on us visibly in an actual radiance.[17]

We all want security. Our ultimate security is founded on God and on him alone. The way this relates to our actual living is to see the process of dying (which begins in our twenties), as much as our physical growth, as a means whereby God makes us ever more transparent to himself. This means that in every situation God can be discovered and the increasing hold of his love can be experienced. Teilhard de Chardin expresses it sublimely in this prayer:

> It was a joy to me, O God, in the midst of the struggle, to feel that in developing myself I was increasing the hold that you have upon me; it was a joy to me, too, under the inward thrust of life or amid the favourable play of events, to abandon myself to your providence. Now that I have found the joy of utilizing all forms of growth to make you, or to let you, grow in me, grant that I may willingly

consent to this last phase of communion in the course of which I shall possess you by diminishing in you.

After having perceived you as he who is "a greater myself", grant , *when my hour comes*, that I may recognize you under the species of each alien or hostile force that seems bent upon destroying or uprooting me. When the signs of age begin to mark my body (and still more when they touch my mind); when the ill that is to diminish me or carry me off strikes from without or is born within me; when the painful moment comes in which I suddenly awaken to the fact that I am ill or growing old; and above all at that last moment when I feel I am losing hold of myself and am absolutely passive within the hands of the great unknown forces that have formed me; in all those dark moments, O God, grant that I may understand that it is you (provided only my faith is strong enough) who are painfully parting the fibres of my being in order to penetrate to the very marrow of my substance and bear me away within yourself.

The more deeply and incurably the evil is encrusted in my flesh, the more it will be you that I am harbouring – you as a loving, active principle of purification and detachment. The more the future opens before me like some dizzy abyss or dark tunnel, the more confident I may be – if I venture forward on the strength of your word – of losing myself and surrendering myself in you, of being assimilated by your body, Jesus.

You are the irresistible and vivifying force, O Lord, and because yours is the energy, because, of the two of us, you are infinitely the stronger, it is on you that falls the part of consuming me in the union that should weld us together. Vouchsafe, therefore, something more precious still than the grace for which all the faithful pray. It is not enough that I should die while communicating. Teach me *to treat my death as an act of communion*.[18]

NOTES

1. John Mortimer, *Clinging to the Wreckage*, Penguin 1982, p. 185.

2. Oliver Warner, *William Wilberforce*, Batsford 1962, p. 154.

3. Stevie Smith, "Come, Death"(2) in *Collected Poems*, Allen Lane 1975, p. 571.

4. *The Guardian*, 20 July 1983.

5. C. J. Feret, *Fulham Old and New*, Vol. I, 1900, p. 266.

6. Dylan Thomas, "Do not go gentle into that good night" in *The Oxford Book of Twentieth Century English Verse*, ed. by Philip Larkin, OUP 1973, p. 474.

7. D. H. Lawrence, "Song of Death" in *The Complete Poems*, Vol. II, p. 723.

8. Harry T. Moore, *The Priest of Love: a life of D. H. Lawrence*, Penguin 1976, p. 629.

9. D. H. Lawrence, "Shadows" in *The Complete Poems*, Vol. II, p. 726.

10. Austin Farrer, *Said or Sung*, Faith Press 1960, p. 13.

11. W. B. Yeats, "Sailing to Byzantium" in *The Oxford Book of Twentieth Century Verse*, ed. Philip Larkin, OUP 1973, p. 82.

12. John 21:18.

13. Sonnet 146.

14. Romans 8:28.

15. *East Coker* II.

16. H. A. Williams, *The True Resurrection*, Mitchell Beazley 1972, and Fount Paperbacks 1983, p. 145.

17. Malcolm Muggeridge, "Credo" in *Jesus Rediscovered*, Fount Paperbacks 1969, p. 178.

18. Teilhard de Chardin, *Le Milieu Divin*, Fount Paperbacks 1964, p. 89.

FOR DISCUSSION

1. What benefits, if any, do you see in "the radical insecurity" of life?

2. Should old age "burn and rave at close of day"?

3. How is it possible – is it possible? – to recognize God under "each alien or hostile force" as Teilhard de Chardin believed?

7.

Love

Love as a Hint and a Symbol

We seek happiness; and therefore we seek love. For it is, above all, love that we most ardently desire. The word *love* conveys the idea of one all-consuming relationship with another person; but it is love that we are looking for from the cradle to the grave. When we are born and turn our face to our mother's breasts it is love we thirst for as much as milk. When we are dying and hold out our hand it is love we want from the person who holds it, even if that person is a near stranger. Nevertheless, it is "falling in love", romantic love, that occupies so many imaginations. Nothing could be more understandable, for this is the condition:

> Where each asks from each
> What each most wants to give
> And each awakes in each
> What else would never be.[1]

This love is an ecstasy, a state of self-transcendence brought about not by discipline but by emotions outside our control. It brings fulfilment, for all our psychic energies are alive and our whole being is doing what it most wants to do. It brings, if not continuously, a sense of peace, security and success. It blesses us with all the aspects of happiness discussed earlier within an over-all ecstasy or loss of self. In short, it brings happiness; or seems to.

Most people over a certain age realize that a person can

"fall in love" many times in the course of a life. They have a practical problem, how to banish or control this state or how to reconcile its working out with acknowledged obligations. Yet in one way their problem is less than that of the person who thinks that falling in love is a once-in-a-lifetime experience; for although when a person is "in love" that love seems the most important thing in the world, no relationship remains at that level of emotional intensity. The problem for someone who falls in love convinced that this is "the real thing" is that this love gets invested with an absolute quality.

The experience of many parish priests is that those who come to get married, far from thinking lightly of marriage as the popular myth suggests, ask too much of it. Someone in his or her teens, or even older, is inclined to think that if only they can meet the right person all their inner discontents and frustrations will be banished. All the quarrels with parents, all the hang-ups of one kind or another; all these will fade away in the joy of one total relationship. There are other factors also which lead people today to have unreal expectations of human relationships in general and of marriage in particular.

First, as a matter of fact, marriage in history has been an economic unit as much as anything else. Still today in many parts of the world you can see husband and wife in the fields together sowing or making hay. Working long hours, with endless hard toil, the couple is better able to survive as a unit than if each was on their own. Since the eighteenth century people have increasingly looked to the marriage relationship for emotional satisfaction. Earlier reasons for marriage, such as property settlements amongst the nobility and wealthy classes, gave way to the desire for a fulfilling relationship. This is good, it is an advance. Yet, when for most of history, and in much of the world today, marriage has been about so many other things beside personal fulfilment, and these other factors have helped to keep the marriage together even if the level of emotional satisfaction was low, it is foolish to isolate the emotional strand and ask it to bear the whole weight of a lifetime's commitment.

Secondly, people today are being asked to live together for far longer than in any other period of history.[2] The average life expectancy of a marriage two hundred years ago was about fifteen years. The usual pattern was for the wife to die in childbirth after having delivered about ten children. The average life of a marriage now, even when one in three is likely to end in divorce, is nearly twenty years. So all married couples today have a challenge that only a few had to face before: how to sustain and deepen a relationship over the whole life span and through all its different phases.

Thirdly, there are all those factors like easy divorce, the dispersal of the extended family, urbanization and the changing role of women, which we are all aware of and so which need not detain us, but which together mean that the social pressures on people to stay together and make a go of their relationship are now very weak. Almost everything depends on the emotional bond between the couple and their mutual care for any children they have.

Fourthly, there is still a facile optimism around about our essential goodness. Or, if we know we have nasty, selfish, spiteful bits of us, we think that if only we had the right person to love, the right relationship, all would be changed and there would be sweetness and light for ever and ever. But, as Auden put it, "We have to love our crooked neighbour with our crooked heart" and that neighbour includes our spouse. The Church used to teach the doctrine of original sin, a doctrine difficult to understand and, as sometimes stated, impossible to believe. But there was and is this to be said for it. It stops people having unrealistic expectations about their own and other people's behaviour. It alerts us to the possibility that even when we are most deeply in love the love may not be as flawless as we like to think.

Fifthly, there has been a decline in the belief in God. For most of Christian history people took it for granted that this life did not offer too much in the way of happiness and that we were here being prepared for an eternal happiness to be found in God. No doubt this led, as Marx and others said, to too little being done to improve human conditions, to a too easy resignation with things as they are. But today, with the decline in religious belief, in particular with the way an expectation of heaven no longer conditions the lives of most people, we expect happiness now. This is not an unworthy expectation, indeed this book is written on the assumption that the desire for happiness is a perfectly proper one; but the present state of religious belief means that people tend to invest their whole hope of happiness in human relationships. That which in the past men expected only of God, they now look for in one perfect human relationship. In short, many people are looking for salvation from a human love, the salving of all their ills, a purpose and meaning for their life and an object to whom they can devote themselves totally. No human relationship can bear this strain. We are asking our fragile human love to give us what only God himself can give; to bear what only God can bear.

The love that is present when people fall in love has an absolute quality about it; it demands to be put first, demands that everything else, every other obligation, gives way before it. In this it reveals a demonic quality, for it is claiming an absoluteness that belongs truly only to God himself. For this reason love is, as Dante said, "A Lord of terrible aspect". Yet, properly understood, this aspect of love points beyond itself. In Evelyn Waugh's novel *Brideshead Revisited* Charles Ryder reflects on his love for Julia:

Perhaps all our loves are merely hints and symbols;

vagabond-language scrawled on gate-posts and paving stones along the weary road that others have tramped before us; perhaps you and I are types and this sadness which sometimes falls between us springs from disappointment in our search, each straining through and beyond the other, snatching a glimpse now and then of the shadow which turns the corner always a pace or two ahead of us.[3]

Julia does not like this reflection when Charles tries to explain it to her. She thinks he is talking about leaving her to find someone else. But he is not talking about an ideal human love; he is pointing to love beyond our human love. In the end it is Julia who acknowledges the claims of this other love and who breaks the relationship with Charles because of it.

I've always been bad. Probably I shall be bad again, punished again. But the worse I am, the more I need God. I can't shut myself out from his mercy. That is what it would mean; starting a life with you, without him. One can only hope to see one step ahead. But I saw today there was one thing unforgivable . . . the bad thing I was on the point of doing, that I'm not quite bad enough to do; to set up a rival good to God's.[4]

Our human loves point beyond themselves to that "Love Divine, all loves excelling". Although what has been discussed here is that falling in love which tends to lead to marriage, there is that passionate friendship between members of the same sex and of the opposite sex which carries the same touch of the absolute. When Stella died Dean Swift was devastated and wrote to a friend in the following words:

Dear Jim,

Pardon me, I know not what I am saying, but believe me that violent friendship is much more lasting and as much engaging as violent love.

All our human loves point beyond themselves to God himself. Cardinal Hume makes the point with simplicity and clarity:

In what does happiness consist? It consists in wanting things and having these wants satisfied. And what is this but to say that happiness consists in loving and being loved! Complete happiness – that for which we were made and the only one that can satisfy consists, therefore, in loving God and being loved by God.[5]

Love Human and Divine

Our longing for love finds its proper focus and fulfilment in the love of God: God's love for us and our love for him. In this relationship of mutual love, which partakes of the relationship of Jesus with his heavenly Father, a relationship which in turn mirrors the relationship within the Blessed Trinity between the Eternal Son and the Father, is to be found our perfect happiness. Yet, for us, questions inevitably arise.

First, for most people this love of God seems so unreal compared to human love. If another human being loves us we experience their warmth. The love of God is so intangible, at best it seems a fleeting emotion, at worst an exercise in deception, something drummed up from inside ourselves. Even the most devout people feel this. Even the most devout people have been known to throw up husband or wife, children, home, job and other obligations, to go and live with someone whom they have come to love. Clearly this love has been more real and powerful for them than the love of God. So what can we say? Simply that some people, however few, have clearly known the love of God as an overwhelming reality. Julian of Norwich, for example, writes about God's love in terms which express experience and carry conviction:

"What, wouldst thou know thy Lord's meaning in this thing? Know it well. Love was his meaning. Who sheweth it thee? Love. Wherefore sheweth he it thee? For Love. Hold thee therein. Thou shalt know more in the same, but thou shalt never know other therein, without end."

Thus was I learned that love is our Lord's meaning. And I saw full surely in this, and in all, that before God made us, he loved us. Which love was never slaked, nor ever shall be. And in this love he hath done all his works. And in this love he hath made all things profitable to us. And in this love our life is everlasting. In our making we had beginning: but the love wherein he made us was in him from without-beginning. In which love we have our beginning. And all this shall we see in God without end.[6]

Few know the reality of God's love in the way she did; yet we have all been put on the road to know it. We are on the way. We have been made of the earth, earthy; and also of heaven, heavenly. We have been made to grope our way forwards, growing through experience, into a greater and greater awareness of God's love.

Secondly, being suspicious moderns we cannot help suspecting that talk about God's love is a compensation for a lack of human love. We wonder whether, if a person was truly fulfilled in a human relationship, they would still hanker after something more. Many of the people who attend church are widowed or divorced or single. It sometimes happens that in middle age a person starts to get interested

in religion and this coincides with a period when their
marriage has become emotionally thin or difficult. These
facts have to be faced and can be faced. For it is undoubtedly
true that we project onto God a great deal of ourselves,
including our starved emotions, if they are starved. This is
inevitable. If God is real and God is a love greater than we
can imagine, we will bring to him and focus upon him all that
we are, including our frustrations. This would happen
whether God existed or not. What matters is that we be as
aware as possible of what we are doing. If we are desperately
lonely and also a devout believer, it would be foolish to think
we do not find some solace for our human loneliness in our
relationship with God. We do; and it is quite right that we
do. It is only dangerous if we try to pretend to ourselves. We
need a robust and down-to-earth self-knowledge of our
emotional needs, which is both humorous and tolerant.

We long for love. What is this love for which we yearn?
It is not a word that we can ever exhaustively define and this
is because it is absolutely central to our religion. "God is
love." The word love must therefore be as mysterious and
elusive as the word God. Nevertheless we can correct one-
sided understandings of the nature of love. One such is that
which equates love and unselfishness. This is deeply
engrained in the Protestant consciousness, and in so far as it
is theologically grounded derives in recent times from a
famous book by the Swedish theologian Anders Nygren,
Agape and Eros.[7] Eros is not a sensual love, but Nygren
regards it as fundamentally different from and opposed to the
agape of the New Testament. Eros is rooted in longing and
desire. It recognizes value in things and leads the self to go
on looking until it finds the source and standard of all that
is true and beautiful and good in God himself. In contrast to
this Nygren sets agape, which begins with God, not man.
Agape does not recognize value, but bestows it. And it is not
man seeking a way to God but God coming down to us,

taking hold of us and enabling us to love others. What Nygren affirms about agape is true but what he denies to Christian love, in excluding eros from it, is false. We can see how this is so in any human love, for example that of a grandmother for her grandchild. The grandmother not only wants the well-being, safety and development of her grandchild. She wants the grandchild to be with her, she enjoys her company. It would be very odd if someone said to us, "I'll do anything to help you except actually want you or want to be with you." "Wanting" has a place in our human loves, an essential place, and so it does in God's love for us. God wanted us enough to create us in the first place and he still wants us enough to come amongst us and die for us that we might be with him for eternity.

Nygren is also wrong in thinking that love only bestows value rather than also recognizing it. We want to be valued for ourselves not to be treated as the object of someone else's loving disposition. Someone once remarked that his idea of hell is to get old and be greeted by his Christian name by an unknown young person on a first visit. What applies in our human relationships is true in our relationship with God. He not only bestows value on us by dying for the ungodly. He recognizes a value we already have by virtue of his creation of us. He is not like someone mentally holding her nose whilst coldly dishing out soup to a down-and-out. Beneath our grime and stink and squalor he can still see a human face and recognize it as what Helen Oppenheimer calls "an irreplaceable centre of minding".

Furthermore, it seems odd that we have been created with a longing for love and happiness if this has no place in the divine love. It makes more sense to think that if God has created us with an eros love it is an aspect of his love for us and our love for him. Divine love includes both wanting us and wanting our well-being. Christian love results from being caught up in this love, a love which overflows from the cycle of loving in the Blessed Trinity. It is a love which finds its fulfilment in a mutual giving and receiving, not in a one-sided giving or a one-sided receiving.

> . . . each asks from each
> What each most wants to give.

Nevertheless, having established that eros love has a proper place in both divine and human love we can then go on to affirm the centrality, on any Christian view, of God's love for us. This love reaches us in many ways. It is, above all, the love revealed in Christ, crucified, risen and living with us now. This love is present with us when we pray and feeds us through the sacraments. This is a love which lies about us all the time, if we could be aware of it. One of the delights of focusing our longing for the absolute upon God, where it belongs, rather than on a single human relationship, is that we are freed to experience love in many ways. Monica Furlong makes the point well when she writes on how to come through a broken love-affair:

> In the first place our expectations about love are somehow askew, curiously distorted by all sorts of fallacies about romantic love. Even when we deny it we secretly often believe that there is one perfect love waiting for us somewhere (a belief which I begin to suspect has more to do with serious gaps in the mothering we originally received than anything to do with life and human affection as it is actually constituted). If there was some perfect love which supplanted all others, we would be desperately distorted people, deprived of the wonderful and amazing variety of human love. We love and need a vast range of affectionate human contacts – this one because she/he feels a bit like a mother or father to me, that one because he/she feels like a daughter or son. This one speaks the accents

of the village I grew up in, that one shares my passion for the ballet. That one is a wonderful drinking companion and tells the sort of risqué story I appreciate. This one lives with a style and elegance that I find fascinating. This one is a kind soul-mate to whom I could confide anything, that one is the sexiest thing I've ever seen. That one is deliciously funny – we do nothing but giggle. This one is the most fascinating gossip in the world and the only way I can keep up with the news in my professional field.

None of these thises and thats, of course, are the "loved one" whose removal costs me such intolerable pain, but if I forget that all the others are there, offering me their own unique gifts of love and joy and naughtiness and fun then already I am on the road to despair, battering my tiny fists against a world that will not gratify my immense wishes in toto.

So one way back from the desert of lost love, from being given a stone from the person from whom one asked bread, is to recognize the depth of love in all human contact.[8]

Philip Larkin has a poem in which he describes a queue of people lining up before an American faith healer for healing. Suddenly he realizes that everything is wrong.

> In everyone there sleeps
> A sense of life lived according to love.
> To some it means the difference they could make
> By loving others, but across most it sweeps
> As all they might have done had they been loved.
> That nothing cures.[9]

This is a pessimistic poem. Yet it is true there are people who have never been loved in the way they long for. There are people who have to live with an open wound. Yet Christianity never pretended differently. It also remains true, however, that there is a divine love which, if we are open to it, reaches us in many ways, expected and unexpected. It may not come in the form we have been looking for, but in one way or another God's love reaches us.

Prayer involves opening the eyes of our mind and heart, and often our physical eyes too, that we might see the love that is lying about us. People who feel that the world is always against them are described as paranoid. They are suspicious that others are getting at them, that the universe is hostile. We don't have a name for the opposite condition, partly because it is not a disease and partly because it does not, alas, exist very often, if at all. Few people go out into the day imbued with a sense that the world is on their side, that love is streaming into them from every encounter, in every sight and in every silence. Yet it is, if we were but more aware. Someone once joked that when in doubt he always took everything as a compliment. This could lead to smugness and illusion; yet it does keep paranoia at bay and it points to the more serious way in which we could be more receptive to the good-will, affirmation and enhancement that plays upon us all the time, if we could but be aware of it.

Dance, my heart! dance today with joy.
The strains of love fill the days and the nights with music,
and the world is listening to its melodies:
Mad with joy, life and death dance to the rhythm of this
    music.
The hills and the sea and the earth dance. The world of
    man dances
in laughter and tears.[10]

Something Lovable in Every Person

Prayer involves, first of all, opening the mind and heart to receive. It also involves searching out what is lovable in the people about us. As Cardinal Hume put it:

> Love is a primary reality: before it is a human fact love exists in God. Remember that we love people because they are there, but with God it is the other way round: because he loves them they are there. This is an important truth because it means there is something lovable in all that has been created. It means there is something lovable in every person; if it were not so, that person would not have been created. It is our task to look for whatever is lovable in others.[11]

There is something lovable in every one. One surprising testimony to this is at funerals. People almost invariably try to find something nice to say about the departed. They may have disliked, despised or hated their guts when they were alive. Yet few are prepared to say "Thank God he (or she) has gone!" They try to find *something* about the dead person which they can affirm. If we can do this when a person is dead, there is no reason why we cannot do it before they die. There is, as a matter of fact, something lovable about every person, for they only exist because God loves them. Our task is to see: to see what Gods sees; to see in them what God sees in them; what is truly in them because God created them.

We are conditioned by our culture to think that love is an emotion that sweeps over you and about which you can do very little either to stop it or to strengthen it. In contrast to this Western idea it is good to set the rather different ideal that comes from the Indian subcontinent. There, still, marriages are often arranged. Yet this does not preclude the development of a genuine love between the two partners. There is a beautiful film by Sanjit Ray in which the hero finds himself married to someone physically unattractive, and how a sensitive and tender relationship grew up between them.

144

Love

In a novel by Salman Rushdie, Amina Sinai loses her first husband, whom she loved, and has to marry someone else. She still thinks about her first husband:

> You ask: what did she do about it? I answer: she gritted her teeth and set about putting herself straight . . . bringing her gift of assiduity to bear, she began to train herself to love him. To do this she divided him, mentally, into every single one of his component parts, physical as well as behavioural, compartmentalizing him into lips and verbal tics and prejudices and likes . . .
>
> Each day she selected one fragment of Ahmed Sinai, and concentrated her entire being upon it until it became wholly familiar; until she felt fondness rising up within her and becoming affection and, finally, love. In this way she came to adore his over-loud voice and the way it assaulted her eardrums and made her tremble: and his peculiarity of always being in a good mood until after he had shaved – after which, each morning, his manner became stern, gruff, businesslike and distant; and his vulture-hooded eyes which concealed what she was sure was his inner goodness behind a bleakly ambiguous gaze; and the way his lower lip jutted out beyond his upper one; and his shortness which led him to forbid her ever to wear high heels . . . "My God," she told herself, "it seems that there are a million different things to love about every man!" But she was undismayed. "Who, after all," she reasoned privately, "ever truly knows another human being completely?" and continued to learn to love and admire his appetite for fried foods, his ability to quote Persian poetry, the furrow of anger between his eyebrows . . . "At this rate," she thought, "there will always be something fresh about him to love; so our marriage just can't go stale." In this way, assiduously, my mother settled down to life in the old city.[12]

This emphasis on what it is possible for us to contribute to love is not in any way to denigrate the emotional element. Furthermore, as Western psychologists will warn us, we cannot pretend with our emotions. We cannot force ourselves to feel what we don't feel. But in the humorous passage from Salman Rushdie, the lady in question seems quite well aware of what she is doing. She does not pretend that his voice is anything but over-loud or that his bad moods are other than bad moods. Yet she does achieve a genuine love for her husband.

Not long ago a woman achieved a certain notoriety for answering an advertisement from a man about to leave for a deserted island who wanted a woman to live with him. In order to get to the island the couple had to get married. When they arrived the woman took off all her clothes and from there on refused to sleep with her husband, a fact that the national press seized on. Less noticed was the fact that in due course, partly as a result of the shared struggle of the man and his wife to stay alive, she admitted to coming to love him. She had responded to the advertisement of a complete stranger, come to dislike him intensely and then, as she said, come to love him in a completely different way.

This is not to say that we should totally separate loving and liking, which the Church has been prone to do. They are more closely linked than has often been preached and both are, to some extent, at once outside our control and within it. As Helen Oppenheimer has written:

> We may well discover that it is no more difficult after all to try to like than to try to love. People do learn to like things. We talk about acquired tastes. When people refuse even to try garlic, we call them faddy. When they are sure they cannot like people, we call them prejudiced. The conviction that one cannot be expected to like, only to love, is defeatist.[13]

Helen Oppenheimer points out that the fact that Christ was a friend of gluttons and winebibbers, the fact that disreputable people liked him and he liked them, shows that liking was part of his love for them. "Worldly people are not inclined to respond to condescension, however divine. It is not unmotivated acceptance but friendly appreciation that warms hard hearts and makes people want to be less selfish and more human."[14] When we are urged to love our enemies we are not being asked to disavow our friends nor is there any suggestion that this is either a different or a better form of love. Rather, the implication is that enemies are to be drawn into the same kind of relationship that we have with our friends. We must begin, suggests Helen Oppenheimer, by *noticing* those we don't like, in particular noticing their special individuality and attending positively to it. Christian love may transcend natural liking but it need not repudiate its origin in ordinary human feelings.

> Friendliness and willingness to like are only a small start towards any kind of human love, but they are a start and a better start than dogged dutifulness. With many of our human neighbours we shall never, in this world, get further than the start, but at least we can look around us in hopeful expectation.[15]

Love and Prayer

Prayer is an expansion of our loving, as Eric Abbott used to say. Even more than that: prayer and love are so closely intertwined that it is almost impossible to separate them. To love someone means having their happiness in mind; means not only wanting them but wanting and genuinely desiring their well-being. How is this possible without prayer? We are so self-centred; so selfish. What we call our love is so shot through with spite and splinters of malice. The closer the relationship we have with someone, as mother or father or husband or wife or lover or close friend, paradoxically, the more this will be so. For it is in close relationships, where there is a genuine bond, that both our positive and our negative feelings emerge. We are polite with strangers. With someone we love we both hug them and shout at them; or most people do. Our flawed, partial feelings for other people can only grow into deep love, can only include a genuine desire for their well-being, in prayer. If this is so in close relationships, how much more so is it true of those to whom we are little drawn? It is prayer, reflecting on the person before God and in God, that enables us to see that which is lovable in them. It is prayer that enables us to affirm them, to build them up rather than cast them down. It is prayer that enables us to see the other person not simply in terms of well-being but of blessedness; for the person we are called to love is someone we are called to help grow into their full stature as a child of God.

Praying and loving are related in a whole variety of ways. One element of prayer consists of meditation on God's love for us shown in Christ, a love renewed through daily contact. This reflection on and imbibing of God's love for us both purifies our human love and draws it to its proper object, God himself. St Augustine believed that there is a thirst for God in all of us but that *superbia*, pride, enters in, so that we are tempted to become self-sufficient. In order to win our love to its proper object God humbles himself and comes amongst us as a man.

To cure man's superbia God's Son descended and became humble. Why art thou proud, O man? God has for thy sake become humble. Thou wouldst perchance be ashamed to imitate a humble man; imitate at least the humble God.[16]

Reflection on God's love for us draws our love towards its proper object and keeps it steadfast. For there is a prideful reluctance in us to be on the receiving end, even of God's love. In a well-known play set in a hospital at the end of the last war a soldier was dying of kidney disease. All the other soldiers in the ward knew this, and as an expression of their desire to care, to be of use, used to offer him their cigarettes. The dying soldier used to reply, in his Scottish accent, "I hae my own". It is God's humility that disarms such an attitude and enables us to receive what we most want, God's love. It is this love that enables us to love others. St Augustine was never tired of quoting Romans 5:5, "The love of God hath been shed abroad in our hearts through the Holy Spirit which was given unto us."

St Augustine began from an eros love, a love rooted in our need and desire for what is of value. This kind of love, as was argued earlier, is an important aspect of true Christian love. Yet it is not the whole. Within all true love there is a miracle so that we not only want the other person, but genuinely want their well-being. This miracle is the work of a lifetime's prayer.

St Bernard of Clairvaux is our best guide here, and thinks of four stages of love. First of all we love ourselves. Then we love God for what we receive from him. We go on to love God for his own sake, and finally we come to love even ourselves for God's sake, a state that St Bernard envisaged happening in its fullness only in heaven. It is not necessary on this scheme to think that eros love, our love based on our need, should be discarded. It is not a ladder that has to be kicked away once we have reached a higher level. On the contrary, all four stages have their place as part of the whole platform. Yet, as St Bernard indicates, a transformation does take place, a miracle, in which our human love is enabled to go beyond itself, both to rejoice in God for his own sake, and to love others with God's own love.

A. N. Wilson's novel *The Art of Healing* explores the nature of love as well as the nature of healing and, rightly, sees the two as most intimately connected. The central character, Pamela Cowper, has a passionate relationship with an American girl, Billy, whom she loves violently. Yet she realizes that it cannot last and that the relationship has not enough substance or depth for it to be prolonged very long. She has also had a long-standing friendship with a fellow university don, John. Yet this relationship did not seem quite right either, though for different reasons.

> Theirs was a friendship, Pamela's and John's, which had depended on a shared conspiracy never to be serious, never to touch the nebulous areas of life about which others feel intensely. It was this, quite apart from the distinctiveness of their own predilections, which had shaped their destiny to the point where a love affair between them would have been unthinkable; for a love affair would have meant, if only momentarily, an agreement to say what they meant without resorting to irony.[17]

This continual resort to irony, which made them such close and mutually amusing friends, but which made it unthinkable for them to say "I love you" seriously, had another cause.

> Beneath the layers of flippancy and irony which life commanded of one, Pamela believed that there was a bedrock of truth. It seemed that John did not share this opinion. As far as he was concerned the layers of half-truth could go on for ever . . . It was the difference between one who considered everything in life to be fluid and

changeable and shifting, and one who searched, however fleetingly, for a point inside or outside what we call life where the motion and the half-truth ceased and the truth could be seen in stillness and face to face.[18]

This led Pamela to look for a love different from that which Billy or John had offered, "A love which could be serious – which yet admitted all her own incurable ironies – that was it. A love which was not solemn but which exalted kindness above everything."[19]

Pamela finds this love in an old clergyman, nicknamed "Sourpuss". Sourpuss is realistic, and caustic, and this, combined with a foul temper, brings the nickname. Yet he is real, both in himself and in his faith. There is no sentiment and much down-to-earth kindness. Pamela marries him and they move to a country vicarage.

She has learnt how to be happy. It is an art. For her, it consists in having plenty of things to cram into the day: research and teaching, which used to occupy so much of her consciousness, are now pushed to the borders of life. Cooking has become a delight: so has the garden (three acres); a little carpentry, early bed, a little visiting the aged. The day is structured; early rising, early bed, hardly an hour which feels "free". She has learnt not to be touchy: one person in a household being touchy is quite enough. Others possibly ask how *can* she be married to a man who loses his temper at such slight provocation? Others do not know that he worships her, and that living with a devotee is the greatest of life's compensations. Others have no sense of what he was like before. The outbursts of anger now merely punctuate life, they do not infuse the whole of it.[20]

For some this will seem too much the happy ending, an

ending which they would regard as eminently privileged
compared to the drabness of their own life, and few, it must
be admitted, are married to someone who could be described
as a "devotee". Our situations are all so different, some
married, others not, some with friends, others lonely. We
cannot generalize from the description of Pamela's life to that
of others – except in one respect. Happiness, like love, is an
art. She has learnt how to be happy. In that art prayer is not
simply an element; it is an essential.

✠

We hold in your presence, O Lord,
all those we love and those who love us.
Your love is so much greater than ours
and you work unceasingly for our well-being,
With all the resources of infinite wisdom and patience.
Bestow on them the fullness of your blessing.

Heavenly Father,
give me a genuine love for others,
both those I like and those I don't like;
help me to overcome my fears and prejudices
and to see your image in all men.

O Christ who welcomed the downtrodden,
those made to feel small,
help us to enlarge others rather than diminish them;
to build up rather than to belittle.

NOTES

1. "The Annunciation" in *Selected Poems* by Edwin Muir, Faber 1965, p. 41.
2. See Lawrence Stone, *Family, Sex and Marriage in England, 1500–1800*, Harper & Row 1980.
3. Evelyn Waugh, *Brideshead Revisited*, Penguin 1962, p. 288.
4. *Brideshead Revisited*, p. 324.
5. Basil Hume, *Searching for God*, Hodder & Stoughton 1983, p. 223.
6. Julian of Norwich, *The Revelations of Divine Love*, chap. 86, Trans. J. Walsh, Burns & Oates 1961, p. 209.
7. A revised edition was published by SPCK in 1953 and 1982.
8. "Jemmy Grove and Co" in *Christian Action Journal*, Spring 1981, p. 7.
9. "Faith Healing" in *The Whitsun Weddings*, Faber 1971, p. 15.
10. Kabir, the weaver mystic of Northern India, is claimed by Hindus and Muslims. The translation is by Tagore. Quoted in *God of a Hundred Names*, ed. Barbara Greene and Victor Gollancz, Gollancz 1962, p. 248.
11. *Searching for God*, Hodder & Stoughton 1977, p. 181.
12. Salman Rushdie, *Midnight's Children*, Picador 1982, p. 68.
13. *The Hope of Happiness*, p. 125.
14. ibid, p. 137.
15. ibid, p. 136.
16. Quoted by Nygren, p. 473.
17. *The Art of Healing*, Penguin 1982, p. 218.
18. ibid, pp. 238f.
19. ibid.
20. ibid, p. 269.

FOR DISCUSSION

1. Do you think that the love described in the New Testament – agape – is the only kind of love that matters to a Christian?

2. Is happiness an art? If so, in what does it consist?

3. Is it true that there is something lovable in everyone?

Acknowledgements

The author is grateful for permission to use the extracts from the works of other authors which are quoted in the text. Publication details are given in the relevant notes at the end of each chapter.

Also available in Fount Paperbacks

Journey for a Soul
GEORGE APPLETON

'Wherever you turn in this inexpensive but extraordinarily valuable paperback you will benefit from sharing this man's pilgrimage of the soul.'

Methodist Recorder

The Imitation of Christ
THOMAS A KEMPIS

After the Bible, this is perhaps the most widely read book in the world. It describes the way of the follower of Christ – an intensely practical book, which faces the temptations and difficulties of daily life, but also describes the joys and helps which are found on the way.

Autobiography of a Saint:
Thérèse of Lisieux
RONALD KNOX

'Ronald Knox has bequeathed us a wholly lucid, natural and enchanting version . . . the actual process of translating seems to have vanished, and a miracle wrought, as though St Teresa were speaking to us in English . . . his triumphant gift to posterity.'

G. B. Stern, The Sunday Times

The Way of a Disciple
GEORGE APPLETON

'. . . a lovely book and an immensely rewarding one . . . his prayers have proved of help to many.'

Donald Coggan

Also available in Fount Paperbacks

The Mind of St Paul
WILLIAM BARCLAY

'There is a deceptive simplicity about this fine exposition of Pauline thought at once popular and deeply theological. The Hebrew and Greek backgrounds are described and all the main themes are lightly but fully treated.'   *The Yorkshire Post*

The Plain Man Looks at the Beatitudes
WILLIAM BARCLAY

'. . . the author's easy style should render it . . . valuable and acceptable to the ordinary reader.'   *Church Times*

The Plain Man Looks at the Lord's Prayer
WILLIAM BARCLAY

Professor Barclay shows how this prayer that Jesus gave to his disciples is at once a summary of Christian teaching and a pattern for all prayers.

The Plain Man's Guide to Ethics
WILLIAM BARCLAY

The author demonstrates beyond all possible doubt that the Ten Commandments are the most relevant document in the world today and are totally related to mankind's capacity to live and make sense of it all within a Christian context.

Ethics in a Permissive Society
WILLIAM BARCLAY

How do we as Christians deal with such problems as drug taking, the 'pill', alcohol, morality of all kinds, in a society whose members are often ignorant of the Church's teaching? Professor Barclay approaches a difficult and vexed question with his usual humanity and clarity, asking what Christ himself would say or do in our world today.

Also available in Fount Paperbacks

BOOKS BY C. S. LEWIS

The Abolition of Man

'It is the most perfectly reasoned defence of Natural Law (Morality) I have ever seen, or believe to exist.'

Walter Hooper

Mere Christianity

'He has a quite unique power for making theology an attractive, exciting and fascinating quest.'

Times Literary Supplement

God in the Dock

'This little book . . . consists of some brilliant pieces . . . This is just the kind of book to place into the hands of an intellectual doubter . . . It has been an unalloyed pleasure to read.'

Marcus Beverley, Christian Herald

The Great Divorce

'Mr Lewis has a rare talent for expressing spiritual truth in fresh and striking imagery and with uncanny acumen . . . it contains many flashes of deep insight and exposures of popular fallacies.'

Church Times

Also available in Fount Paperbacks

The Sacrament of the Present Moment
JEAN-PIERRE DE CAUSSADE

'It is good to have this classic from the days of the Quietist tensions with its thesis that we can and must find God in the totality of our immediate situation . . .'

The Expository Times

The Poems of St John of the Cross
TRANSLATED BY ROY CAMPBELL

'Mr Campbell has recreated the extraordinary subtlety of the music of the original in an English verse worthy of it and that climbs from aspiration to ecstasy as if it were itself the poem.'

The Guardian

Thérèse of Lisieux
MICHAEL HOLLINGS

A superb portrait of one of the most popular of all saints.

'This book is well worth recommending . . . presents a simple factual outline of Thérèse's life and teaching . . . (with) incidents . . . applied to our own everyday lives.'

Review for Contemplatives of all Traditions

I, Francis
CARLO CARRETTO

This unusual and compelling book is a sustained meditation on the spirituality of St Francis of Assisi, bringing the meaning of his message to our time.

'A book one will not forget.'

Eric Doyle, The Tablet

Fount Paperbacks

Fount is one of the leading paperback publishers of religious books and below are some of its recent titles.

- ☐ THE QUIET HEART George Appleton £2.95
- ☐ PRAYER FOR ALL TIMES Pierre Charles £1.75
- ☐ SEEKING GOD Esther de Waal £1.75
- ☐ THE SCARLET AND THE BLACK
  J. P. Gallagher £1.75
- ☐ TELL MY PEOPLE I LOVE THEM
  Clifford Hill £1.50
- ☐ CONVERSATIONS WITH THE CRUCIFIED
  Reid Isaac £1.50
- ☐ THE LITTLE BOOK OF SYLVANUS
  David Kossoff £1.50
- ☐ DOES GOD EXIST? Hans Küng £5.95
- ☐ GEORGE MACDONALD: AN ANTHOLOGY
  George MacDonald C. S. Lewis (ed.) £1.50
- ☐ WHY I AM STILL A CATHOLIC
  Robert Nowell (ed.) £1.50
- ☐ THE GOSPEL FROM OUTER SPACE
  Robert L. Short £1.50
- ☐ CONTINUALLY AWARE Rita Snowden £1.75
- ☐ TRUE RESURRECTION Harry Williams £1.75
- ☐ WHO WILL DELIVER US? Paul Zahl £1.50

All Fount paperbacks are available at your bookshop or newsagent, or they can also be ordered by post from Fount Paperbacks, Cash Sales Department, G.P.O. Box 29, Douglas, Isle of Man, British Isles. Please send purchase price, plus 15p per book, maximum postage £3. Customers outside the U.K. send purchase price, plus 15p per book. Cheque, postal or money order. No currency.

NAME (Block letters) _____

ADDRESS _____

_____

_____